Railway Signalling Track Plans

Bob Essery

Ian Allan
PUBLISHING

Front cover: Running under clear signals, ex-LNER 'J27' 0-6-0 No 65814 is framed by the signals at the north end of the platform that dominate this August 1965 picture taken at Seghill on the old Blyth and Tyne line, which became part of the North Eastern Railway and later the LNER. The advantage of the engine and brake working is that the brake van can be propelled. *John Edgington*

Back cover, top: This picture was taken at Welsh's Bridge Signalbox, Inverness in July 1655 and shows the 6.25am express passenger train from Helmsdale hauled by Class 5 No 44788. Normal practice at Inverness was for trains to run past and then set back into one of the platforms in order to assist cross platform traffic. *John Edgington*

Back cover, bottom: At first glance it is difficult to see that this is a model. The picture was taken on the Hillingdon Railway Modeller's splendid 7mm finescale scale layout set at East Dean. As with so many realistic models this is not a real location, but a 'might have been'. This rewarding approach to modelling does require considerable research into what a company might have constructed and how it would have been operated. *Photographer*

Title page: I have always felt that good trackwork, be it on the full-size railway or on a model, should 'flow'. This picture, taken from the roof gantry at London's Cannon Street station in November 1958, illustrates what I mean. Although I doubt if many modellers would even contemplate the construction of anything approaching this in model form, the concept of 'flowing trackwork' can be seen very clearly. The problem is that unless you construct your own track you can only use the limited range of 'ready-to-run' formations, which restricts the potential for interesting designs. *Martin Welch*

First published 2007

ISBN (10) 0 7110 3215 7
ISBN (13) 978 0 7110 3215 6

Published by Ian Allan Publishing

an imprint of Ian Allan Publishing Ltd, Hersham, Surrey KT12 4RG
Printed by Ian Allan Printing Ltd, Hersham, Surrey KT12 4RG

Code: 0703/

Visit the Ian Allan Publishing website at
www.ianallanpublishing.com

Contents

Preface   3

Introduction   4

1 Historical Review of the Development of Permanent Way and Track Formations   8

Overview   8

Permanent way in detail   12

Glossary of trackwork terms   33

2 Historical Review of the Development of Signalling   34

Running signals   42

Subsidiary signals   52

Colour light signals   59

Telegraph poles   64

3 Operating the Railway   66

A brief summary of some Requirements that could apply to modellers   66

Working the line   87

Working of single lines   87

4 Signal Stations   93

Development of signal boxes   93

Other signal stations   105

5 A Modeller's Viewpoint   110

Appendix 1: Summary of Legislation   112

Appendix 2: References and Sources   112

Preface

A little more than four years have passed since I completed the introduction to what is affectionately known as 'Operation One', or, to use its correct title, *Railway Operation for the Modeller*. When the idea was put to the publisher, I do not think anyone could have foreseen that three additional titles would follow, but this is the fourth, or, to use the working title, 'Operation Four'. When this series began, the original objective was to provide modellers with a single source of reference that would help them to avoid some of the basic errors that can be seen when visiting almost any model railway exhibition; however, this initial aim has grown somewhat, and additional books dealing with specific subjects were requested. But that might beg the question, why should that be necessary? This is only a hobby – does getting it right really matter? In order to respond to anyone who takes this view, it may be helpful to explain my reasoning, and thus reset the scene for the series.

I was very lucky to have been old enough see the final years of the steam railway and to spend some time working in that environment. There can be little doubt that railways, both full-size and in miniature, have played a very important part in my life, but the Victorian steam railway is no more. As mentioned previously, railway preservationists do a remarkable job, but they can only provide a flavour of the railway system of yesteryear. On the other hand, accurate models can show in some detail what they were like and how they were operated. For this reason it is most important that those who present their work in public – be they authors who write about historical railways or modellers who show their work in three-dimensional form to the public – produce as accurate a picture as possible.

The question is, what is meant by 'accurate'? It must be acknowledged that there is a large element within the hobby that is not really interested in reproducing in miniature an accurate representation of railways, but would rather seek enjoyment from watching the models run. While this approach is fine, it does not enable the maximum potential enjoyment to be obtained from the hobby; however, I freely accept that not everyone shares these views, and the subject is discussed further in Chapter 5.

In an ideal world the starting point would be for everything to be dimensionally accurate, and while to a degree this is possible, we cannot, for example, make the figures on our layouts move in a lifelike fashion. Therefore we are into the realms of compromise, and in a way these operating books are designed to show first how the railways were operated during what is known as the steam era, and second to provide some ideas that modellers may use to enhance their layouts.

As technology improves we might find that what is considered impossible today may become commonplace in the future. For example, at one time two-rail electrification was considered by most of the leading figures in the hobby to be unworkable, and fierce arguments raged for a number of years about the pros and cons of two-rail versus three-rail. When Hornby introduced two-rail models and ceased to sell three-rail, that was the end of the debate in 4mm scale, although it took many years for the message to sink in with many Gauge O modellers. Therefore I take the view that, while today some aspects of the prototype cannot be reproduced in miniature, who knows what the future may hold? The biggest problem – perhaps challenge would be a better word – is the question of length, or distance, between two locations. Not many of us have the space we need to accurately display the prototype, and the larger the scale we adopt the more difficult this becomes – an example is the length of a train. Therefore the intelligent use of space is a key element of railway modelling.

In writing this book I am as always conscious of the help that I have received from my friends, and I would begin by acknowledging the assistance received from Richard Chown, who has allowed me to quote from his informative paper 'The Board of Trade Requirements', published by the ScaleSeven Group in 1997, which provided me with the idea behind the theme for this book. Others who have helped are Phil Chopping and Roger Stone, for their help with sourcing certain signalling material; Richard Davidson, for early signalling information; John Edgington, who was able to supply a number of pictures and made many useful comments; Tony Overton, for his advice over the years about signalling; Martin Welch BSc (Eng) CEng MICE, whose advice on permanent way was most constructive; and Tony Wright, courtesy of *British Railway Modelling*, for supplying the pictures of the models featured in the book. Finally I must thank Graham Warburton for his very considerable input on various aspects of signalling, and his numerous suggestions to improve the text, so much so that at times it was almost a joint effort. I am most grateful to all for their unstinting help with this project.

Bob Essery
Rolleston on Dove
2006

Right: The track at the approach to major stations was usually complex, and this 1959 view of the departure side of Euston underlines this. Note the congested arrangement of points and crossings, including non-standard units. The message this picture provides is simple: if you have a large station on your layout the trackwork will generally look more realistic if you introduce a 'congested' look. *Martin Welch*

Introduction

When planning the structure of this book I was reminded of the well-known conundrum of the 'chicken and the egg', and which came first, but if you adopt the same approach to track and signals the answer is neither. The railways of Britain were built by private capital and the investors expected to receive dividends from the revenue that was generated by the transport of passengers, goods and minerals. Therefore the starting point for railways is traffic, real and perceived. Some lines were of a defensive nature and were built to counter incursions by one company into the territory of another, but even so the basis for their construction was to protect the owning company's income from the existing traffic.

If that argument is accepted, the sequence was first the potential traffic, then, in order to move it, the construction of the railway. As the traffic developed it had to be controlled or regulated, and as a result signalling systems were developed. The early railways were rather primitive, but the development of the railway system during the early Victorian period was rapid and covered many aspects of engineering, some of the most fascinating of which were in the realms of signalling and train control. Generally, but not entirely during the period under review, signalling was of the 'semaphore' type, although colour light signals have been used for many years. One form of signalling that has lasted since the very beginning of railways is hand signals, and, as we will see, they are particularly appropriate for modellers.

During a lifetime's study of railways I have formed some conclusions that I would like to share with readers. My early full-size railway experiences during the late 1940s and early 1950s provided first-hand experience and a basic understanding of how the railway was worked, but this was only a starting point. Although I began railway modelling in the late 1940s, it was not until 1956 that I embarked upon what has been more than 50 years of continuous involvement, beginning with 4mm-scale OO wheel and track standards. At first the period modelled was the early British Railways scene, and I can still remember being pleased that, modelling this era, I did not have to try to produce gaily painted private-owner wagons! By 1960 the writings of Norman Eagles influenced my thinking, and as a result the move back in time began, at first to the LMS, circa 1937, but thereafter all changes of period have been the direct result of my own research.

The years spent researching LMS locomotive and carriage livery in conjunction with the late David Jenkinson convinced me that the pre-Stanier period was most attractive, and later I became convinced that the pre-Grouping period had much to offer, not least

Below: The stimulus to build railways was the potential for investors to profit from the transport of passengers and goods, which until then had travelled by stagecoach, packhorse or canal, by offering a better service. In order to illustrate 'traffic' I offer this picture of the Midland Railway goods station at Lawley Street, Birmingham. It is almost timeless, and could be a scene from the Victorian or Edwardian period – only the motor lorry provides a clue to its early-1920s date. Goods were packed in crates, barrels, bales and boxes, and generally the mixture of traffic seen here would not have been out of place during the final years of the steam era. *Author's collection*

Above: Uppingham was a former LNWR station at the end of the short branch from Seaton in Rutland. Most modellers tend to use a signal box when modelling this type of station, but as we can see the levers – there appear to be nine – were in a frame on the platform. I presume that the man in charge was graded as a Porter Signalman. The train is interesting: the locomotive is motor-fitted Ivatt Class 2MT No 41321, but it is hauling the Motor Driving Trailer rather than propelling it – the driving compartment is at the end of the coach coupled to the engine. *Author's collection*

Below: This c1960 view of Tewkesbury shows some interesting features that could be seen during the British Railways period. The Midland station was on the branch from Ashchurch to Malvern, which later became part of the Western Region. Therefore while the Midland station lamp and LMS Hawkeseye station nameboard are in keeping, the GWR upper-quadrant signal is an example of something that could happen when former LMS stations came under Western Region control. Note also the barrow crossing and footpath, the latter running alongside the line and separated from it by a fence. *D. Ibbotson*

that everything on wheels was smaller and occupied less space, which for most modellers is rather useful in view of the problem of length mentioned above. It was the need to understand the earlier years of railway history that led me into the fascinating hobby of research, which has almost become a separate hobby in its own right.

For this reason I can never understand why modellers use the term 'modeller's licence', which suggests that they are guessing and cannot be bothered to get it right. In your own home or on a club layout I do not object, but if you take your models to an exhibition, where they can influence others, I think modellers should aim for historical accuracy. In making this statement I recognise that I must exclude the vintage three-rail or tinplate layouts often seen at exhibitions, or those built by youngsters who are starting in the hobby – but at the specialist society exhibitions I would expect to see very high standards.

The problem is that, if errors are made, others may copy what you have done, and thus the mistakes are

multiplied. So how are these mistakes to be avoided? The answer is simple: study the prototype and follow the rules. In my view a modeller who wants to create 'realism in miniature' must begin by understanding the rules that governed both the construction and operation of the full-size railway and follow them. In my experience I have found that when modellers adopt this approach, generally their understanding, interest and enjoyment increases enormously.

The British railway system was built in accordance with what became legal government requirements embodied in Acts of Parliament. Some of these Acts came about as a result of accidents or the need to improve the way the railways were regulated. In 1840 the Board of Trade Railway Department was set up, and this body had an immense impact upon the way the British railway system developed during the years that followed. Over the years successive Acts of Parliament provided the Board of Trade with the authority it required, and these Acts are summarised in Appendix 1. The fact that the railways of the British

Isles were built and operated within a legal framework cannot be overstated. If modellers ignore this, it could be argued that they commit an absurdity. For example, if you go to a football match you will not expect the players and referee to make up the rules as they go along. By not working to the 'rules for railways', there is a danger of not getting the maximum enjoyment from the hobby. We also miss out on making our layouts that much more interesting by failing to fit them out to meet the operating requirements of the period being modelled and all the things that we want to achieve in our model of a section of railway.

In previous books on railway operation I have suggested that the 1889 Regulation of Railways Act was most important, and that 1890 was roughly the pivotal point in steam railway history. The Regulations under the 1889 Act led to the publication of a comprehensive set of Requirements by the Board of Trade in 1892, the earliest version having been published in 1858. Re-issued at various times, since 1950 in blue covers, hence the name 'Blue Book', they were extended to cover matters such as electrification and automatic level crossings. In 1996 they were replaced by a new document, *Railway Safety Principles and Guidance*, published by HM Railway Inspectorate (HMRI) of the Health and Safety Executive.

As UK legislation for railways is not retrospective, for quite a number of matters, such as platform heights, so long as there has been no change on the ground since their original approval of construction there is no call to change them to meet current Requirements. There may of course be a need to change to meet public unease, or to allow new rolling-stock to run – but any such change is subject to HMRI approval. In making this point I have gone beyond my 1968 end-of-steam-traction cut-off date, simply to show that railway history is continuous and that sometimes it is very helpful to know the origin of what happened and how it developed. This is particularly true if a modeller wishes to build historically accurate models.

The Requirements can have a number of possible consequences for modellers. A chosen prototype may have significant operational restraints that make it less interesting than it appears; this may be because the owning company installed equipment and procedures to achieve the versatility it needed, but which may not be quite what the modeller is seeking. On the other hand the modeller, by adding the equipment and procedures to achieve the required versatility, can modify a chosen prototype and still remain within the rules. The modeller can also design a layout from scratch and incorporate the desired equipment and procedures while remaining within the rules. Finally, after many years in the hobby, my ideal approach would be to build a model of a real location at a given date. By following this course guesswork is eliminated, and it will often be found that the real location contains operational aspects that are far more interesting than anything that could be invented – but the need to study the prototype takes time that could be spent on making models.

In this book I have tried to follow a logical theme. Notwithstanding my comments about the importance of traffic, a subject covered in some depth in the three previous titles, I propose to begin with an historical review of the development of track and to try to identify many of the component parts that make up the permanent way. Of necessity it will be an overview – my first rough draft revealed that to explore the subject in depth would have taken up too much space, yet just to describe the components used by most

modellers would be too sparse. Nevertheless it should provide modellers with an understanding of how the permanent way was developed and what the various components and formations are.

This is followed by a similar historical review of signalling. Again, what is not attempted is to provide examples of all the signals used by the many companies. Photographs and drawings are used to show the development of signals and to illustrate examples of the various types.

In the third chapter we begin to see how traffic influences the track and signal arrangements, and a number of examples are included to show typical arrangements that could be incorporated into models. The chapter continues by examining how the railway was worked. In view of the number of single-line railways built by modellers, part of Chapter 3 is devoted to exploring how they were operated. On the full-size railway the main lines were by far the most important part of the system, but this is not really true as far as models are concerned. Space, time and financial constraints means that branch lines are particularly attractive to modellers, which is why so many are constructed, usually as single lines.

The fourth chapter is devoted to 'signal stations', a term I use to describe signal boxes, open lever frames on station platforms and ground frames – but again it is only possible to show a representative selection of what was built by the various British railway companies, safe in the knowledge that similar installations existed on most major companies' systems.

Finally Chapter 5 is largely personal and based upon my experience as a modeller who has also been

able to exhibit his work in public. This chapter also includes some notes about hand signals, as they have an important part to play in the hobby.

The final point I would make is to pre-empt any reviewers who might comment, perhaps adversely, upon the abundance of Midland or LMS material. There are good reasons for this: it shows principles that applied to all British railways, and my personal collection of pictures and paperwork is largely from the LMS group of companies. It could also be said that the Midland Railway, my favourite company, was well recorded, probably better than any other pre-Grouping company, and providing its practice was similar or identical to other British companies I think that it makes sense to make use of it.

If there are any errors of fact or omissions of detail, both are entirely my responsibility.

Below: No apologies are offered for including this splendid undated but late-Victorian period picture of the Midland side of Birmingham New Street station. Most days around lunchtime I would cross the bridge while engaged in watching the trains; the station was not far from where I worked before the railway employed me. It was also quite close to the shop in Dale End that supplied me with model railway equipment at the start of my interest in railway modelling. Nostalgia apart, the picture has been included to show how the ballast was laid so that it came almost to the top of the rails. Finally note the platform signal suspended from the footbridge above the rear coach. *National Railway Museum*

Chapter One

Historical Review of the Development of Permanent Way and Track Formations

Overview

Although this statement may not find favour with some modellers, in my opinion the most important part of a model railway is the track, or, as it is also known, the permanent way. Let us begin with the obvious: if the track is not to gauge and not well laid, poor running and derailments will follow, with frustration replacing potential enjoyment. Moreover, as we have seen in my previous books, although the wheel and track standards determine the appearance of the locomotives and stock, we must also ask ourselves whether, even when there is no train in sight, the model looks realistic? Often the answer is no, but this is not the place to debate such matters; instead we will begin with the full-size railway, and look at the pros and cons of model railway track later. Although this chapter is largely devoted to a review of the development of track and the identification of its various component parts, there will inevitably be some overlap with the subject of 'train working' covered in Chapter 3.

Although I take the view that the first 'proper railway' was the Liverpool & Manchester, which opened in 1830, the malleable iron rails that were the hallmark of the early railways had been introduced at Wallbottle Colliery, near Newcastle-upon-Tyne, about 1805, and this marked the beginning of the development of the 'Iron Way'. In the Introduction I said that I would make use of Midland and LMS

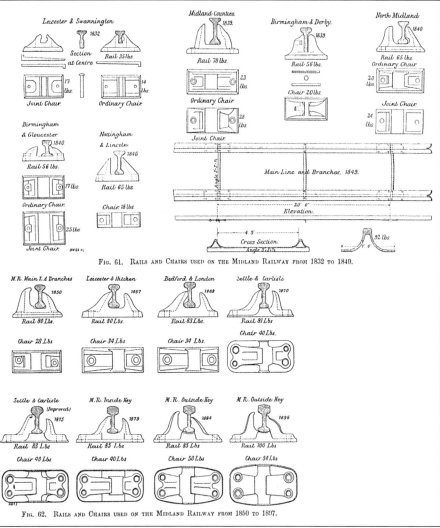

Above left: There is not a train in sight in this commonplace scene from the era of the steam railway. The station is Llanrwst & Trefriw on the former LNWR Conway Valley branch. Photographed in the early 1950s, the photograph contains much to interest modellers. Note that trains approaching from behind the photographer will have a straight run into the platform, with the point connecting the platform loop diverging to the right; the same arrangement applies at the far end of the station. Note the facing point lock between the point blades and the fouling bar alongside the left-hand rail on the approach; the point rodding runs to the signal box seen in the far distance. There is a barrow crossing at this end of the station and we can see the reverse side of the warning boards on each platform. The main station building is to the left, with little more than waiting rooms to the right. The lamps that can be seen are two on each platform; there were probably also two on each platform beyond the buildings. Signalling comprises home and starting signals in each direction, with no doubt other signals controlling the small goods yard.
R. S. Carpenter collection

Left: This extract from the Presidential Address by Samuel Waite Johnson shows the development of Midland Railway track, typical of permanent way in general in Great Britain during the 19th century.

Right: Although the GWR's 'broad gauge' is beyond the scope of the present book, I felt that I should include at least one view of a railway built to a gauge wider than 4ft 8½in. This is a section of the Londonderry Port & Harbour Commissioners' line with a mixed gauge of 5ft 3in and 3ft 0in – quite a challenge for modellers! *Author's collection*

material, and we begin with an extract from the President's Address to The Institution of Mechanical Engineers in April 1898. This address, by Samuel Waite Johnson, the Midland Railway's Locomotive Superintendent, is particularly valuable as being the only published example of this nature known to me. The year 1898 is, as stated before, close to the 'pivotal point' in the history of the steam railway, and in that year Johnson was able to look back to the 1840s when the constituents of the Midland Railway had been operating for just a few years. Therefore, by quoting from his address, the 19th-century developments of one of the major British railway companies may be considered as being fairly typical of what was happening elsewhere throughout the country.

If we start in 1832 we find that when the Leicester & Swannington Railway opened the company was using wrought-iron rails of 'fish-belly' pattern. These were 15 feet in length, fastened by wrought-iron keys into cast-iron chairs, which were spiked to oak sleepers, half round in section – a far cry from what was to come. A few years later in 1839 wrought-iron rails of double-headed pattern were in use on the Midland Counties Railway. The chairs were cast iron, but were spiked down to blocks of Derbyshire millstone grit; use was also made of Kyanised larch cross-sleepers instead of the millstone grit. At this date fishplates had not been invented, so rails were held end to end in special joint-chairs.

The Birmingham & Derby line was also opened in 1839. This company used wrought-iron rails keyed by wrought-iron ball-and-cotter fixings into cast-iron chairs spiked to oak sleepers of half round section. On the North Midland Railway, opened in 1840, wrought-iron double-headed rails were used with cast-iron chairs spiked to timber sleepers, but the Birmingham & Gloucester, also opened in 1840, used flat-bottomed wrought-iron rails spiked to triangular-section sleepers, apex downwards. This company also used half-round-section wooden sleepers, securing the rail in the cast-iron chair by an outside wooden key.

Other systems were also employed, but I have made the point that the development of early railways was somewhat experimental, as the engineers established the best materials for track construction. In 1850 the Midland began to use a round-topped rail on both main line and branches. It was double-headed, the idea being that it could be turned over to increase its life. Produced in 20-foot lengths, it weighed 80lb per yard and was secured to cast-iron chairs using keys, with fishplates at the rail joints.

The next major development was to use rails made from steel; the Midland's Bedford to London line, opened in 1868, originally had wrought-iron rails, but they were later replaced by 83lb per yard steel rails. In this respect the Midland was behind the LNWR, as the latter had laid steel rails in 1862. In 1875 the Midland Improved Settle & Carlisle rail came into service; weighing 83lb per yard and 24 feet in length, the keys were on the flange side of the rail. During the 1960s the late David Jenkinson told me that he had discovered some inside-keyed track still in use on sidings on the line, but I cannot recall the location. What it does confirm is the longevity of rail in sidings that were not subject to heavy use. It also provides me with the opportunity to record that the railways re-used old equipment: main-line rails, chairs and sleepers were often re-used on secondary lines and particularly in sidings after they were considered to be life-expired on the main line.

To bring the story of Midland Railway track to the end of the 19th century, we find that the company introduced 85lb steel rail in 30-foot lengths in 1884, and 100lb steel rail in 36-foot lengths in 1896, but within a few years the rail length for both weights had been increased to 45 feet, both types using cast-iron chairs with outside keys. An LMS document, 'Standard Railway Equipment Permanent Way', dated April 1929 and issued by A. Newlands, Chief Civil Engineer, gives details of the 85lb and 95r BS rail (see below) in use by the company. The document confirms that these were the common weights of rail used at that time and gives the dimensions for crossings between 1-4 and 1-16 with details of switch 'A' (9 feet) to 'E' (24 feet). The temptation to reproduce extracts has been resisted on the grounds that they would have limited appeal, and it would be more beneficial to concentrate on identifying and explaining the use of various track components, then to consider the formations (although many modellers use track that is 'ready made', which tends to reduce the available design options for track formations).

Having reviewed the 19th-century developments, albeit briefly, some readers will have noticed that thus far there has been no mention of either the 'broad gauge' of the GWR or any narrow gauge systems. The reason for apparently ignoring these is simply that they are outside this book's terms of reference. I recognise that Brunel's 'broad gauge' did have far-reaching effects on the GWR, resulting in that company's loading gauge being more generous on lines that had been laid to the 7ft 0¼in gauge, but it proved to be outside the mainstream of British track development. There is a specialist society devoted to modelling the 'broad gauge', and some splendid models have been produced over the years. Likewise, narrow gauge railways are extremely popular with modellers, and many such layouts have been built. An advantage is that they are not demanding as far as space is concerned, and can be used as the sole railway system on the model or as a feeder line to a standard gauge railway, which was the role of several as far as full-size practice was concerned. However, to describe the many variations of narrow gauge would take up too much space, so we will return to the development of Stephenson's 4ft 8½in 'standard gauge' permanent way.

I believe it was in 1889 that the LNWR – 'the Premier Line' – laid the first 60-foot lengths of rail in Great Britain, and later the company was to achieve the reputation of having the best permanent way in the world. During the 20th century further developments took place. In 1905 bullhead-section 95lb-per-yard steel rail was introduced for main-line use, and 85lb steel rail for secondary lines. As a result of work undertaken by a joint committee consisting of representatives from British railway companies, the British Standards Institution and rail manufacturers, the British Standard 95lb-per-yard bullhead rail was first specified in B.S.11 in 1920 and adopted as the common standard for all British railways except the GWR, which had introduced its '00' rail in 1900 (weighing 97½lb per yard) and which it continued to use. In 1922 the 95lb British Standard and the 85lb rail were altered by increasing the head thickness by 1/16in; in order to compensate, the foot was decreased by the same amount. This section was known as the 95lb RBS (also 85 RBS), RBS meaning Revised British Standard, and sometimes shown simply as 85r or 95r.

Other developments may be briefly summarised. Concrete and steel sleepers were introduced, and later welding replaced fishplates on many lengths of line. The most important development from a modeller's point of view was the introduction of flat-bottom rail to replace the traditional bullhead. Although types of flat-bottom rail had been used for many years, it only became more widely used in the UK from about the mid-1930s on main lines. The LMS carried out experiments using flat-bottom rail in 1936, at first using 110lb-per-yard rail. Later experiments made use of 131lb standard American flat-bottom rail, and further trials in 1940 led the way to the adoption of flat-bottom rail to replace bullhead. Finally an early BR decision was to use a completely new section of 109lb-per-yard rail. There were subtle differences to be seen with flat-bottom track, and a number of drawings are included to provide some examples of the fastenings used, while another drawing shows one of the methods used to lay flat-bottom track in concrete or paved areas.

Above left: Concrete sleepers were not widely used in Great Britain, but the Midland & Great Northern Joint Railway was at the forefront in developing the use of concrete for railway purposes, including sleepers. This picture from December 1917 illustrates concrete sleepers laid near Melton Constable. *Author's collection*

Above right: Forty-five years later, in April 1962, the up fast line at Wolverton is being re-laid using prefabricated sections; the Tracklayer, borrowed from the Western Region, is standing on the down fast line. The new track sections are 109lb flat-bottom rail with BJB fastenings and concrete sleepers. *Martin Welch*

Left: This late-1920s picture was taken by the LMS to show steel sleepers that had probably been laid on an experimental basis. *NRM, Derby Collection, DY16015*

Below: No doubt the photographer's attention was on Class 9F No 92110 at the head of a train of loaded hopper wagons on the approach to Rise Hill Tunnel on the Settle & Carlisle line on 29 July 1966, but the reason for its inclusion here is to show the flat-bottom rail that had replaced the bullhead rail used previously. *Paul Cottrell*

Right: This view looking north at Kingsbury in about 1958 shows how the up line, nearest the camera, has been re-laid with flat-bottom rail while the down line retains older bullhead rail. The use of both types on adjacent lines was commonplace, and is something that modellers should consider if they are modelling the 1950s/'60s period or later.
D. Ibbotson

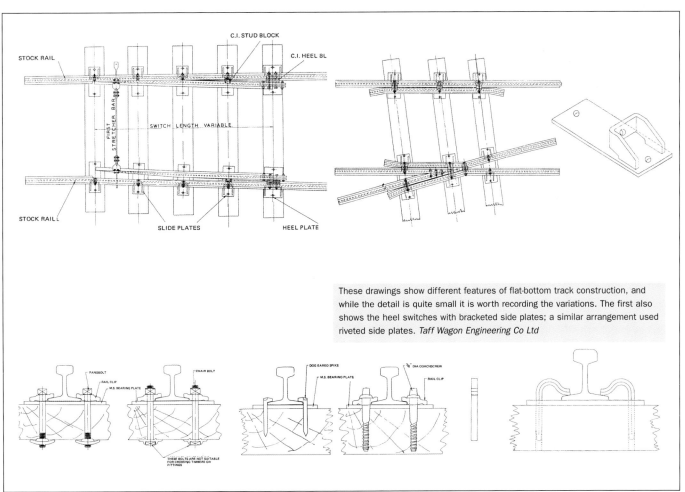

These drawings show different features of flat-bottom track construction, and while the detail is quite small it is worth recording the variations. The first also shows the heel switches with bracketed side plates; a similar arrangement used riveted side plates. *Taff Wagon Engineering Co Ltd*

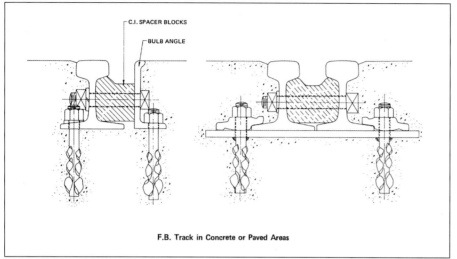

F.B. Track in Concrete or Paved Areas

C.I. SPACER BLOCKS

BULB ANGLE

Permanent way in detail

Be it straight, curved or pointwork, the track is far from the top of a modeller's agenda, so the subtle differences that could and indeed can still be seen on the full-size railway are largely ignored. While it is possible, if making your own track, to use the correct sleeper widths and spacing, the variety of different rail sections that were to be found cannot be reproduced simply because the rail is not available from the trade. Even worse is the very limited variety of types of chair that are obtainable, so an accurate representation of track is consequently difficult. However, things could be a lot worse; when I started to build 4mm-scale track to EM standards in 1960 I used TT flat-bottom rail that was soldered to staples in the fibre sleepers. It was not until a few years later that a reasonable representation of bullhead rail became available from the trade. Until then what was sold for 4mm scale use was too large, and at one time the O gauge modeller had to use rail that was more suited to No 1 and 2 gauges, so matters have improved. Correct sleeper spacing is the most important visible feature, and if this can be achieved then it is possible to obtain a reasonable appearance. It is only the lack of the variety of chairs used with pointwork that is missing.

Fishplates

On both the model and the prototype the weakest point in plain track is the rail joint. Early railways used joint chairs, although other methods included tapering the rails at each end and overlapping the rail joints in the rail. Prior to the introduction of continuously welded track, fishplates were the

Above: Although on a model viewers would not see the rail fixing below the surface of the paved area, I felt that, apart for the fact that the drawing shows how the rail was secured, it also illustrates the clearance for the wheel flange, which may be useful for modellers reproducing this arrangement.
Taff Wagon Engineering Co Ltd

Below: I have included this drawing of London, Tilbury & Southend Railway track in order to show that the sleeper spacing was not even throughout the length of the rail, but was closer together at the point where the rails joined. This principle applied to all railway companies and lengths of rail. During the pre-Grouping period sleepers were 9ft by 10in by 5in, but in about 1920 there was a change, and 8ft 6in became accepted as the standard length, although it took many years before all the 9-foot sleepers were

renewed and replaced. Depending upon company and circumstances, there could also be slight variations in the distance between sleepers, and indeed the number of sleepers per length of rail. Generally 30-foot rail had 11-12 sleepers, 45-foot rail 17-18, and 60-foot 23-24. Extra sleepers, usually two or three, were laid on sharp curves, in tunnels and at water troughs. Crossing sleepers on pointwork were usually 14 and 12 inches wide, and it should also be noted that during the Victorian period some companies used interlaced sleepers on pointwork. The wooden bearers beneath points and crossing work are known as 'timbers'; they used to be softwood, but now hardwoods, typically Jarragh, are used, and the depth is 5 inches. When softwood is used the section is 12 inches wide and 6 inches deep, and lengths between 9 and 24 feet at 6-inch intervals would be employed.
Author's collection

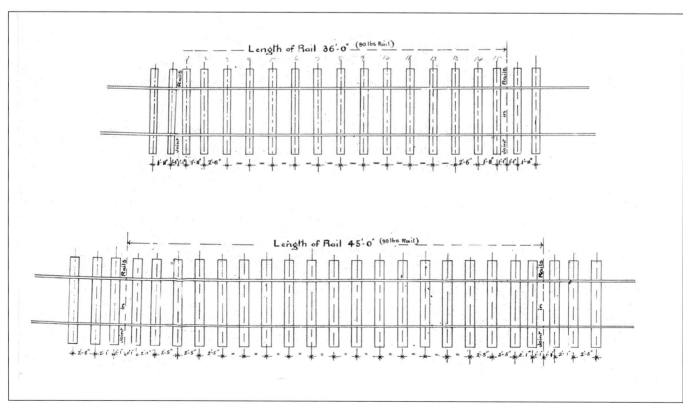

universal method used to join lengths of rail, and they were a Board of Trade requirement; they were metal bars about 18 inches long fitted on each side of the rail joint, with four bolts passing through them and the web of the rail. The accompanying drawing shows the arrangement.

Track formations

The question of track formations was considered in *Railway Operation For The Modeller*, but it is necessary to expand upon what was said there. Although I will try to avoid repetition, it is inevitable that some facts will have to be restated in order to ensure completeness.

In order to maintain a balance between my favoured pre-Grouping period and the later years of the steam railway, I have used drawings and descriptions from the British Railways period to show the different track formations, although historically different descriptions and terms have been used; a good example is 'turnout', which is also known as a 'point', even though 'points and crossing' is more accurate.

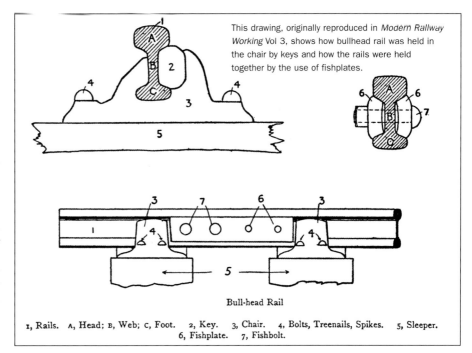

This drawing, originally reproduced in *Modern Railway Working* Vol 3, shows how bullhead rail was held in the chair by keys and how the rails were held together by the use of fishplates.

Bull-head Rail

1, Rails. A, Head; B, Web; C, Foot.   2, Key.   3, Chair.   4, Bolts, Treenails, Spikes.   5, Sleeper.
6, Fishplate.   7, Fishbolt.

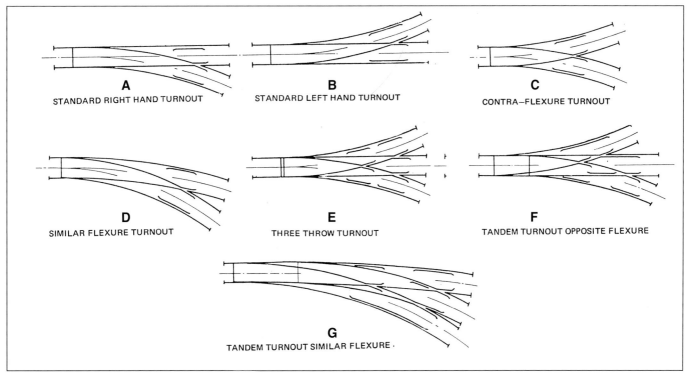

A
STANDARD RIGHT HAND TURNOUT

B
STANDARD LEFT HAND TURNOUT

C
CONTRA–FLEXURE TURNOUT

D
SIMILAR FLEXURE TURNOUT

E
THREE THROW TURNOUT

F
TANDEM TURNOUT OPPOSITE FLEXURE

G
TANDEM TURNOUT SIMILAR FLEXURE ·

Above: These drawings were originally reproduced in an undated but post-1955 Taff Wagon Engineering Co. Ltd catalogue, with some additional comments.

A is a 'Standard right hand turnout', other variations being shown at B, C and F. Some were built with a straight switch and a crossing that could be either straight or curved, and with a true circular curve between the tangential to the switch at its heel and the crossing at its point. For the more subtle variations readers are referred to the technical books listed in the References, in particular *Railway Permanent Way* by Wm Hepworth.

B shows the opposite hand to A, while C is a 'Contra-flexure turnout', which means that two

connected curves bend in opposite directions. A common modelling description for this arrangement is a 'Y point'. D is a 'Similar flexure turnout', where the two connected curves bend in the same direction.

E is a 'Three throw turnout', sometimes called a three-way point and often confused with F, the 'Tandem turnout'. The three-throw is an arrangement of two turnouts with unequal-length switchblades set alongside each other; it is very difficult to model and probably only possible in a scale standard. In the earlier years of the steam railway they could be found on the main lines, but were generally confined to sidings and were only used where space was restricted, although the Midland Railway in particular

made considerable use of them in sidings. A good example of a survivor is on the Keighley & Worth Valley Railway at Haworth yard.

The 'Tandem turnout' (F and G) is also known as a 'Double turnout' and 'Pannier leads', although 'tandem' was probably more commonly used. Note that the switches of the second turnout follow those of the first before a crossing occurs. The advantage of this point was that it saved space, and a succession of tandem points was often the best way of laying a number of sidings from a gathering line. 'Opposite flexure' means that the diverging roads are in opposite directions.

Left: A three-throw point photographed at Cricklewood in 1930. The point was worked by two hand levers at the left hand side, and, using railwaymen's terminology, is set to run through the centre road. As can be seen, each pair of switchblades comprises one long and one shorter blade. The first blade on the left is against the left-hand stock rail and is connected to the third blade from the right. The second longer blade is connected to the shorter second blade from the right, which is against the right-hand stock rail. These turnouts are not easy to model but they save space. Also worthy of note is the drain to the right of the point and the surface of the ground, level with the top of the sleepers. *National Railway Museum*

STANDARD LEFT HAND CROSSOVER ROAD

Left: A 'Standard left hand crossover road'. Assuming that the direction of travel is left to right on the upper line, this is a 'trailing' crossover, requiring a reversing movement; a corresponding right-hand crossover would be 'facing', allowing a train to run over it in the direction of travel. A crossover road consists of two turnouts joined with a connecting portion of track, and can be laid as straight track or on a curve. Another variation would be when one line was straight and the other converged or diverged.

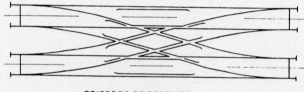

SCISSORS CROSSOVER

Left: A 'Scissors crossover', which might be described as a pair of crossover roads that intersect each other, is sometimes called a 'double crossover'. On the prototype, where space was available, the use of two separate crossovers was preferred on the grounds of lighter maintenance. From a modelling standpoint two separate crossovers are easier to build.

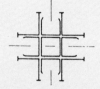

SQUARE CUT THROUGH

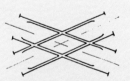

DIAMOND CROSSING

Far left: The 'Square cut through', where two roads crossed at right angles, was not a common arrangement on main lines.

Left: A 'Diamond crossing' is a crossing of two roads at an angle, and is so called from the shape formed by the centre of the crossing.

Left: This two-track diamond crossing, photographed at Widnes Dock Junction in January 1958, would provide a challenge for the most accomplished track builder. we have included an enlargement of the crossing here; the picture on page 112 shows the signal box and other lines in the area. *Martin Welch*

Right: This picture was taken at Waterloo station throat in August 1964 and shows in the centre foreground a single 'outside slip' in 95lb bullhead rail. It forms part of the complex and congested arrangement that was typical of the approach to a major terminus. *Martin Welch*

Below right: A 'Single slip'. A slip road is a connecting track between two other tracks where they cross each other. The use of single or double slips on main lines in the facing direction was avoided where possible on account of the difficulty of providing locking bars. Straight intersecting tracks are best suited for the insertion of single slips, and the flatter the crossing angle the easier the curve of the slip, but single slips were often used on curves. A variation of the single slip is the 'outside slip', which is an arrangement where the switches of the slip road lie outside the 'V' crossings of the diamond. It was not commonly used, but provided a means of forming a slip when the diamond angle was too wide to allow an inside slip to be used.

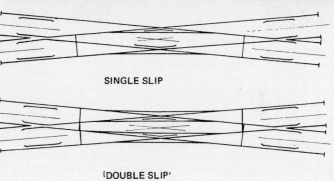

SINGLE SLIP

'DOUBLE SLIP'

Right: In a 'Double slip' the two intersecting tracks are connected in both directions. As with single slips, the use of double slips on main lines in the facing direction was avoided where possible on account of the difficulty of providing locking bars. Again, straight intersecting tracks are best suited for double slips and the flatter the crossing angle the easier the curve of the slip, but double slips were often used on curves.

Right: This rather splendid picture has been included to show a double slip. The location is Saltley station, and the picture was taken from the north end of the island platform. The running line to the right of the signal box is the down main line, and beyond there are up and down goods lines. To the left of the signal box is the up main line, then more goods lines. The line crossing the picture is a trailing connection between the up and down lines, and by constructing a double slip two short sidings between the south end of the signal box and the north end of the station could be made. My recollection is that they were only used to deliver stores, mostly coal, to the signalman and station staff. *Author's collection*

Below: A single junction (or double junction if the dotted lines were laid). Of the two arrangements shown, the double junction was more common and comprises two turnouts, either left-hand or right-hand, and a diamond crossing. The rules to follow are that the line carrying the faster traffic should have the easier curves, and the curves through the points and crossing should be eased as far as possible even at the expense of sharper curves on the plain line beyond.

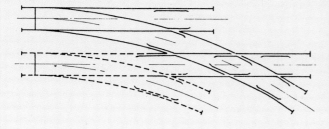

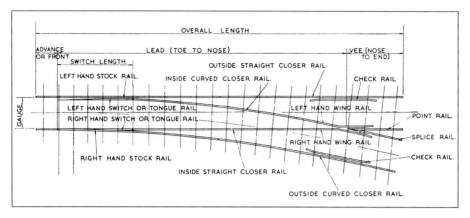

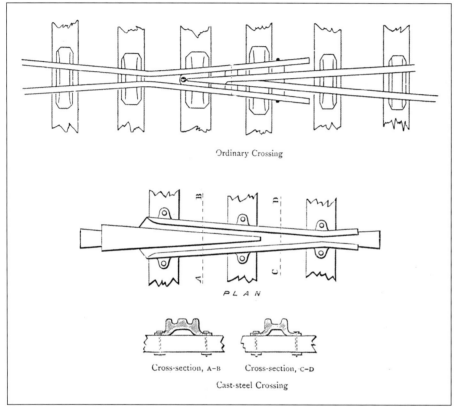

Ordinary Crossing

PLAN

Cross-section, A–B   Cross-section, C–D

Cast-steel Crossing

The turnout is the most common track formation, and can be either left-hand or right-hand; the accompanying drawing (left) is of a right-hand turnout, with all the various components identified. I consider that it is important to use the correct railway terms. Modellers tend to invent names for component parts, then others assume the word is correct. Although not connected with track, a good example is what model wagon-builders call the 'W iron'; this is perfectly acceptable when used to describe a pressing that, when viewed end-on is in the shape of a U with a flat bottom, and viewed side-on is an axleguard. In fact, the component is actually two axleguards held together by a flat base, which was designed by the originators of Protofour in the late 1960s to enable wagons to be compensated. There is no full-size equivalent. Unfortunately some writers now use the term when 'axleguard' is the correct description. On the other hand, alternative names for components were used by different companies, and wherever possible I will draw attention to these alternatives.

Above left: This drawing of a right-hand turnout is included to familiarise readers with the names of the component parts. *Taff Wagon Engineering Co Ltd*

Left: These drawings show a point crossing, which is commonly referred to by modellers as a 'frog'. The first drawing is the more common type and shows a crossing that has been built up from sections of rail, while the other is one that has been cast from steel. In modelling terms this is the most important part of the point, and in my experience, unless you have matching wheel and track standards, this is where you will experience trouble. Too much clearance or 'slop' will ensure a bump or rock as the wheels pass through the crossing, and I have found that the closer to scale the models are the better will be the quality of the running. *From* Modern Railway Working *Vol 3*

Left: Outside contractors supplied the component parts to the railway companies and this picture, taken in May 1958, shows part of the yard at Taylor Bros of Sandiacre, where units are being assembled. Note the 1 in 7½ common crossing in the foreground and the obtuse crossing to the right. Taylor Bros usually supplied units with the chairs and base plates attached. *Martin Welch*

Right: This drawing is based upon a sketch by Martin Welch and is designed to show the difference between 'common' and 'obtuse' crossings, which are defined by their angle, for example '1 in 8'. ('Obtuse' is from the Latin word indicating an angle of more than 90 and less than 180 degrees, while 'common' is 'commonplace', or most frequently used.) The longer the leads the flatter the angle. For most sidings and everyday main-line use, a 'B' switch with a 1 in 8 crossing is normal, described as a B.8. Main-line crossovers tend to be C.9, while double junctions depend very much upon the speed desired; a typical arrangement where 25mph was required would be a D.12, while an F.21 would be used if 45mph was the desired speed. Diamond crossings have two common and two obtuse crossings. The obtuse crossings cannot be flatter than 1 in 8 otherwise there is a danger of the wheel flange going the wrong side of the 'nose'. When a flatter angle is required 'switch diamonds' – moveable switchblades – are used.

Right: A 'switch diamond', showing the use of moveable switchblades, moved to suit the direction of travel. This picture was taken at Wilmslow in 1958 and was part of a new installation over a 45mph junction. *Martin Welch*

Below: This picture was taken at Liverpool Exchange on 12 April 1959 and shows the station throat. Note the use of non-standard points and crossings, necessary to enable all the multi-directional movements to be made within the limitations of the site, together with the obtuse crossing in the diamond crossing seen in the foreground. *Martin Welch*

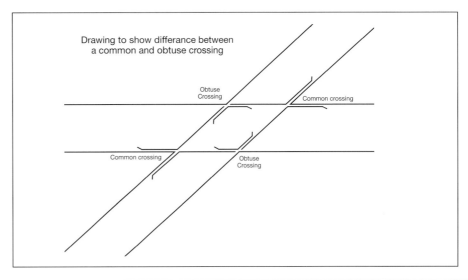

Drawing to show differance between a common and obtuse crossing

Obtuse Crossing

Common crossing

Common crossing

Obtuse Crossing

SETTING OUT DIMENSIONS FOR STANDARD LEADS.

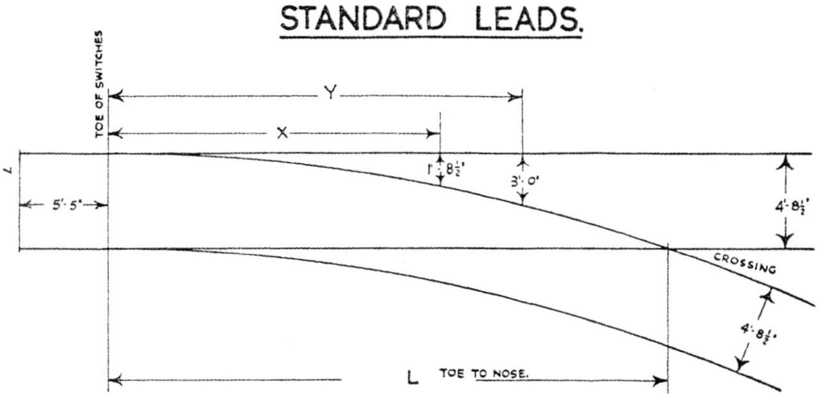

Left: I have resisted the temptation to include tables from the 1929 LMS document 'Standard Railway Equipment Permanent Way', but I believe I should include some details of the 1951 British Transport Commission standards for the home railways. Probably the most useful section for modellers who build their own track, or those who want to know more about the dimensions that applied during the final years of the steam railway and into the post-1968 era, is the section on 'Setting out Dimensions' reproduced here. They represent 109lb flat-bottom rail (bullhead dimensions are similar to an inch or two). 'A' switches were only available in bullhead rail and were not generally used except for sidings where space was tight, so they are not included in the tables. It was normal practice to use crossings in the turnout that provided equal radius of switch and turnout curves, ie A.7, B.8, C.10, D.12, E.16 and F.20.

For Key Diagram, see Page 7.

B SWITCHES

Crossing	X	Y	L Nose of Crossing
1 in 6	34′ 3⅛″	46′ 2¾″	58′ 1⅛″
1 in 6½″	34′ 5⅜″	47′ 1⅝″	59′ 11¼″
1 in 7	34′ 7⅛″	47′ 11¾″	61′ 8½″
1 in 7½″	34′ 8⅞″	48′ 9⅛″	63′ 4⅞″
1 in 8	34′ 10¼″	49′ 5¾″	65′ 0⅜″
1 in 8½″	,,	,,	65′ 2⅜″
1 in 9	,,	,,	65′ 7⅜″
1 in 9½″	,,	,,	66′ 2⅞″
1 in 10	,,	,,	67′ 0½″

C SWITCHES

Crossing	X	Y	L Nose of Crossing
1 in 7	41′ 11″	55′ 9⅝″	69′ 7¾″
1 in 7½″	42′ 3⅛″	56′ 11½″	71′ 9″
1 in 8	42′ 7″	58′ 0⅝″	73′ 9½″
1 in 8½″	42′ 10⅜″	59′ 1″	75′ 9⅛″
1 in 9	43′ 1½″	60′ 0¾″	77′ 8⅛″
1 in 9½″	43′ 4¼″	60′ 11¾″	79′ 6¼″
1 in 10	43′ 6⅞″	61′ 10¼″	81′ 3¾″
1 in 10½″	,,	,,	81′ 5⅜″
1 in 11	,,	,,	81′ 9½″
1 in 12	,,	,,	83′ 0⅛″

Above dimensions are to nearest ⅛″.

For Key Diagram, see Page 7.

D SWITCHES

Crossing	X	Y	L Nose of Crossing
1 in 8	49′ 7⅞″	65′ 6¾″	81′ 4¾″
1 in 8½	50′ 1″	66′ 9⅞″	83′ 7½″
1 in 9	50′ 5¾″	68′ 0⅜″	85′ 9⅜″
1 in 9½	50′ 10⅛″	69′ 2¼″	87′ 10⅝″
1 in 10	51′ 2⅛″	70′ 3½″	89′ 11⅛″
1 in 10½	51′ 5⅞″	71′ 4⅛″	91′ 11⅛″
1 in 11	51′ 9¼″	72′ 4⅛″	93′ 10⅜″
1 in 12	52′ 3⅜″	74′ 2¾″	97′ 7″
1 in 13	,,	,,	98′ 0⅛″
1 in 14	,,	,,	99′ 0⅝″
1 in 16	,,	74′ 5¼″	102′ 6⅞″

E SWITCHES

Crossing	X	Y	L Nose of Crossing
1 in 10	65′ 9″	85′ 10⅜″	105′ 8⅝″
1 in 10½	66′ 2½″	87′ 2⅛″	107′ 11⅞″
1 in 11	66′ 7½″	88′ 5⅜″	110′ 2¾″
1 in 12	67′ 4¾″	90′ 10⅛″	114′ 6½″
1 in 13	68′ 1″	93′ 1⅛″	118′ 8¼″
1 in 14	68′ 8¼″	95′ 2¼″	122′ 7⅞″
1 in 16	69′ 8½″	98′ 11¾″	130′ 1⅝″
1 in 18	,,	,,	132′ 4″

Above dimensions are to nearest ⅛″.

For Key Diagram, see Page 7.

F SWITCHES

Crossing	X	Y	L Nose of Crossing
1 in 12	81′ 11½″	106′ 3½″	130′ 2″
1 in 13	82′ 10⅜″	108′ 11⅛″	134′ 8⅞″
1 in 14	83′ 8″	111′ 4⅞″	139′ 1¾″
1 in 16	85′ 0¾″	115′ 11¾″	147′ 6¼″
1 in 18	86′ 2⅜″	120′ 0⅞″	155′ 4¼″
1 in 20	87′ 1¾″	123′ 8⅝″	162′ 8¼″

Above dimensions are to nearest ⅛″.

Right: This picture, taken in 1958 at Wilmslow, shows an F.20 (45mph turnout) at the junction with the Styal line. *Martin Welch*

Below: This second view of the Styal line junction at Wilmslow, taken in December 1957, shows an 'F' switch 1 in 20 crossing for higher speeds (45mph) just after it had been laid in preparation for electrification. *Martin Welch*

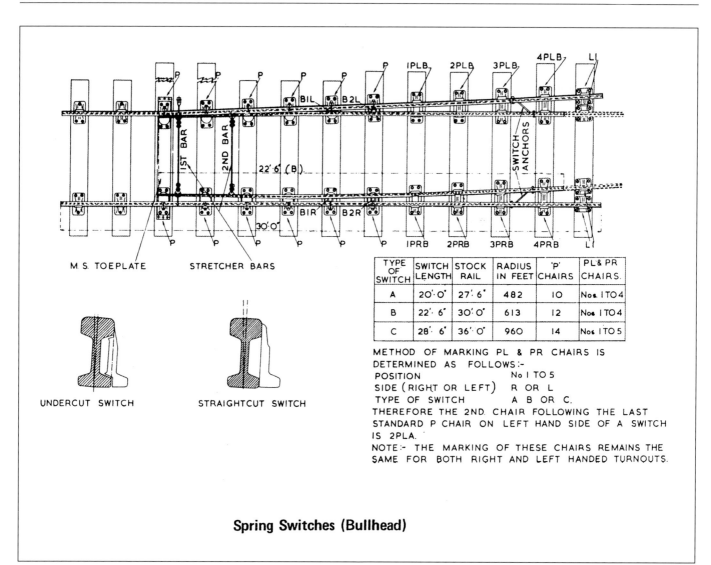

TYPE OF SWITCH	SWITCH LENGTH	STOCK RAIL	RADIUS IN FEET	'P' CHAIRS	PL & PR CHAIRS.
A	20'·0"	27'·6"	482	10	Nos. 1 TO 4
B	22'·6"	30'·0"	613	12	Nos. 1 TO 4
C	28'·6"	36'·0"	960	14	Nos. 1 TO 5

METHOD OF MARKING PL & PR CHAIRS IS DETERMINED AS FOLLOWS:-

POSITION	No 1 TO 5
SIDE (RIGHT OR LEFT)	R OR L
TYPE OF SWITCH	A B OR C.

THEREFORE THE 2ND. CHAIR FOLLOWING THE LAST STANDARD P CHAIR ON LEFT HAND SIDE OF A SWITCH IS 2PLA.

NOTE:- THE MARKING OF THESE CHAIRS REMAINS THE SAME FOR BOTH RIGHT AND LEFT HANDED TURNOUTS.

Spring Switches (Bullhead)

Above: This drawing of the spring switches of a left-hand turnout shows the arrangement of the two stretcher bars, and draws attention to the different length of switch rails, which depend upon the type of switch and the varying size of the 'P' chairs, or, as modellers call them, slide chairs. To the casual observer the main difference appears to be in the arrangement of the chairs. *Taff Wagon Engineering Co Ltd*

It is not unusual to find switches described as 'undercut' or 'straightcut'. The accompanying drawing (above) shows the difference between them, and also illustrates the position of the 'stretcher bars', often referred to by modellers as 'tie bars'. 'Stretcher bars' is correct, and they are usually attached to the 'drive bar' – a 'tie bar' is something different. For example, on the full-size railway a tie bar was used by the permanent way gang as a temporary repair when the gauge started to spread on a curve, usually as the result of faulty or rotting sleepers; the bar was a length of steel rod about 1 inch in diameter, threaded at each end with nuts and washers, and it held the track to gauge until permanent repairs could be made, such as replacing the sleepers. (A permanent tie bar, or tie rod, can be seen in the drawing of rails set into a paved area. See page 22.)

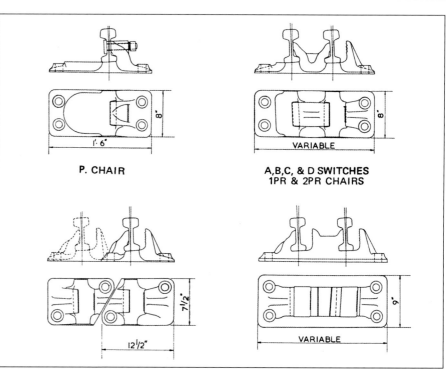

Note also the shape and size of the various chairs. As I have said, modellers are not well served in this respect, but it is understandable. Apart from the distinctive designs used by various companies, the chairs came in numerous shapes and sizes to suit the points. Although what I call 'running rail chairs', or more correctly 'common chairs', are available from the trade, together with what are known as 'slide chairs', the various special chairs, in either functional or cosmetic form, are generally not available. In my view this is due to the number of options that would have to be supplied if a full range was to be made available, together with the fact that the majority of modellers are less concerned about the finer aspects of track. The accompanying drawings together with some of the pictures reproduced in this chapter, will give some idea of the variety of chairs in use on the full-size railway.

Right: I have mentioned the lack of variety of chairs available to the modeller from trade sources, but this is probably because chairs were designed to suit different weights of rail as well as to individual company designs, so the permutations of design are very considerable, as seen in this selection of drawings taken from the Taff Wagon Engineering Co Ltd catalogue. *Taff Wagon Engineering Co Ltd*

Below: Checkrail chairs for the up Birmingham line on the Rugby flyover are seen in this photograph taken in April 1962 The 95lb RBS rail has been laid, but awaits the checkrails. Note that the special chair (SIC) holds both the running rail and check rail. *Martin Welch*

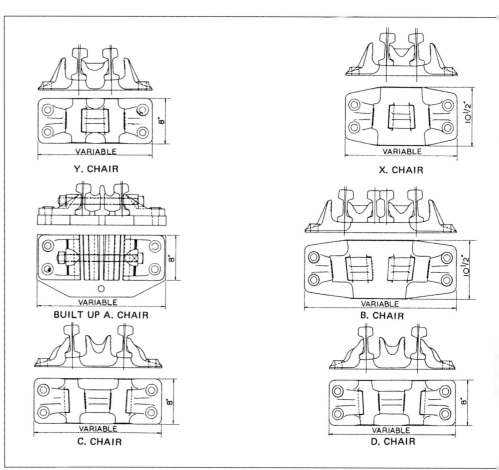

Y. CHAIR

X. CHAIR

BUILT UP A. CHAIR

B. CHAIR

C. CHAIR

D. CHAIR

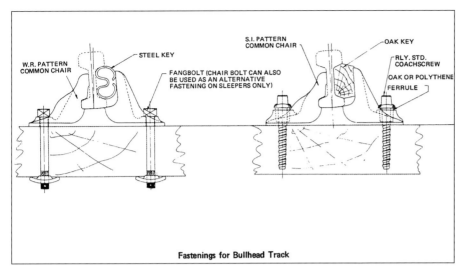

Fastenings for Bullhead Track

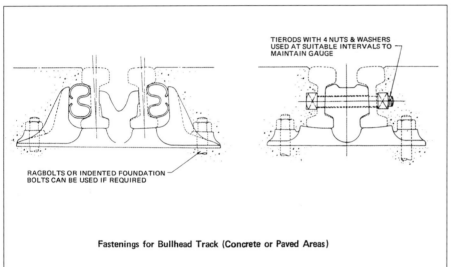

Fastenings for Bullhead Track (Concrete or Paved Areas)

Although wooden keys to hold the rail in the chair were used for many years, steel keys were in use on the LNWR in 1864, but many years were to elapse before they were in general service on the British railway system. The accompanying drawing (left) shows both steel and oak keys and how the 'common chair' was fastened to the sleeper. I have also included a drawing (centre left) showing the arrangement for paved or concreted areas up to rail level. The majority of modellers do not appear to make use of this arrangement in their goods yards, and while the drawing shows how the rail was fixed in place the important thing is the finished effect as seen in the photograph (below left). I have found that the use of Dass modelling compound enables very realistic paving or granite setts to be formed such as were commonplace in goods stations and elsewhere when it was necessary for road vehicles to come alongside rail wagons.

Above left: Drawings showing how chairs for bullhead track, using both wooden and steel keys, were fastened to the sleepers. *Taff Wagon Engineering Co Ltd*

Left: Drawings showing how bullhead track was used in concrete or paved areas. In modelling terms this drawing is also intended to make the point that the road surface should come up to the top of the rail, an arrangement used where road vehicles crossed over sidings in goods stations. *Taff Wagon Engineering Co Ltd*

Above right: I have included this view of the interior of the London Brighton & South Coast Railway engine shed at Newhaven in order to show the usual arrangement of track inside a running shed. Note that the entire area is 'paved' – the material used would vary from place to place, but the surface would generally be at or almost at rail level. This allowed barrows to be wheeled across the lines and made it more convenient for the men working in the shed. Engine pits were usually continuous and ran from end to end other than where access between the roads was required. *NRM, F. Burtt collection*

Left: Although taken at Derby St Mary's goods station in 1918, apart from the rolling-stock this picture could be from the 1950s/60s. It illustrates that in many areas where road vehicles came alongside rail wagons the area was paved to allow the vehicles to cross the lines. The setts were usually raised slightly to enable the rainwater to run away, although no drains can be seen in this view. I use Dass modelling clay and different punches to mark out the lines of the setts, which vary in size, those seen here being rather small. *Author's collection*

Super-elevation

Few modellers employ super-elevation on their layouts, but when it is used there is no doubt that the appearance of a train leaning into the curve is well worth the effort. Super-elevation is achieved by raising the outer rail of a curve to form a cant and thus counteract centrifugal force. The mathematics determining the height of the outer rail is quite complicated, but the outer rail could be up to 6 inches higher than the inner one. Generally super-elevation was not used through points and crossings, but if a junction was located on a curve it would be necessary. Closely associated with super-elevation are transition curves, which I have already mentioned; these are also known as an 'easement' and may be described as a curve of constantly changing radius to allow a smooth movement from a straight line to a curve.

Ballast

Ballast is the roadbed on which the permanent way is laid and over the years at least four different systems were employed. The material used has also varied, including crushed slag, limestone, whinstone, granite, gravel, burnt clay and engine ashes. Later practice was to use an angular hard material. The usual specification required stone

Curves

Sharp curves can cause modellers immense problems, and the full-size railways were not immune from similar difficulties, so a brief comment will not be out of place. Modellers often use reverse curves where tracks are diverted to run alongside a platform, or when connecting two adjacent tracks. On the prototype a length of straight track was usually laid between the two reverse curves, the length depending upon the space available and the speed of the traffic; if possible a transition curve would be used. Modellers are usually restricted for space, but the length of straight track needs to be at least the length of the longest fixed wheelbase, although the length of the longest vehicle would be better.

Buffer-locking is the most common problem encountered with sharp curves and it is interesting to see how the prototype dealt with the problem, using solutions that could also apply to the model: flatten the curve, to make a gradual change from straight to curve; increase the width of the buffer faces of the vehicles that buffer-lock; and prohibit vehicles with an excessive overhang of buffer faces beyond the wheels. An interesting note in the permanent way manual from which the above was taken is worth repeating, that the calculations do not allow for the slightly increased tendency to buffer-lock due to the play of the wheels between the rails. In other words, if you have a lot of side play, buffer-locking will be more likely. On my layout I have proved to my satisfaction that if there is virtually no side play, buffer-locking does not happen.

Below: This drawing, taken from the June 1925 edition of *The Railway Engineer*, shows four different methods of ballasting track. The earliest method is shown as Fig 1, while the current (1925 and later) is Fig 4. According to the accompanying article, the arrangement shown in Fig 1 dated from the 1860s and Figs 2/3 show later developments as the engineers sought to improve the standards of permanent way in order to cope with increased axle loads and speeds. From a modelling standpoint accurate reproduction of ballast and roadbed does much to enhance a layout, while poor attention to this feature can spoil an otherwise excellent model.

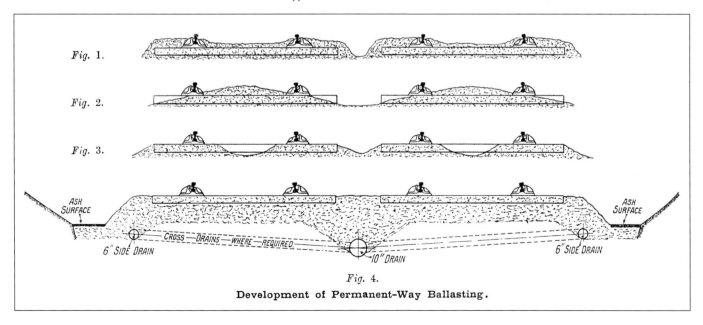

Fig. 1.

Fig. 2.

Fig. 3.

ASH SURFACE   ASH SURFACE

CROSS DRAINS WHERE REQUIRED

6" SIDE DRAIN   10" DRAIN   6" SIDE DRAIN

Fig. 4.
Development of Permanent-Way Ballasting.

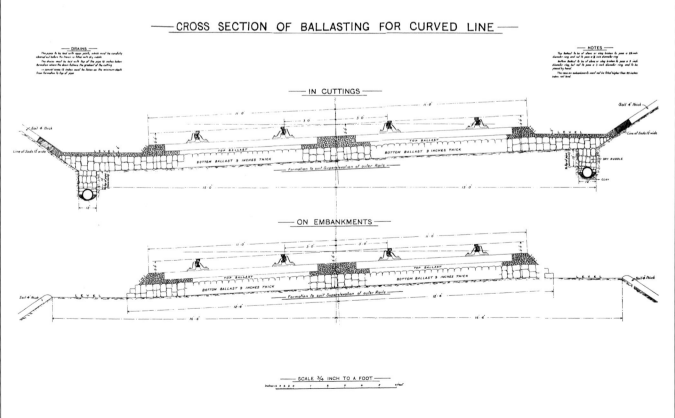

For those modellers who wish to place their railways in cuttings or on embankments, this drawing should be helpful and shows the dimensions that apply. The simple rule is a slope angle of one vertical to one and a half horizontal.

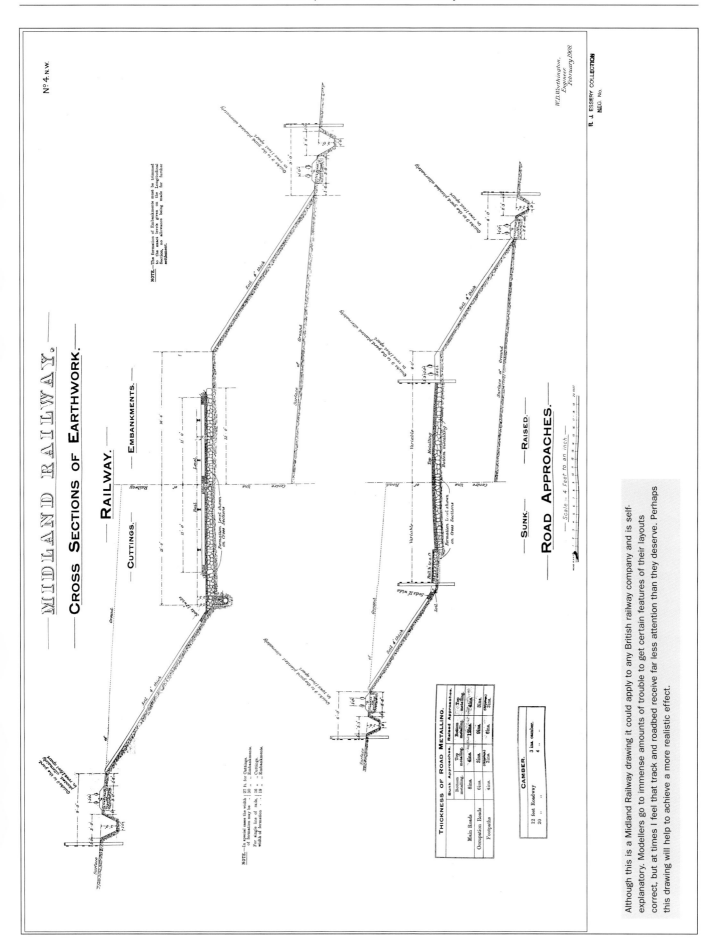

Although this is a Midland Railway drawing it could apply to any British railway company and is self-explanatory. Modellers go to immense amounts of trouble to get certain features of their layouts correct, but at times I feel that track and roadbed receive far less attention than they deserve. Perhaps this drawing will help to achieve a more realistic effect.

graded in size from ⅜ inch to a maximum of 2 inches, with granite being the favoured material, particularly with concrete sleepers. The differences that concern modellers are those that can be seen, and generally the finer points of drainage are of little or no interest. The most obvious visual difference was the way the ballast was laid, and as modellers we should also be careful to get the texture right. Generally modellers tend to use ballast that is too coarse and it is often a good idea to use a finer material. For example, to get what I consider to be the correct appearance I tend to use ballast sold for use by 4mm-scale modellers even though I model to 7mm scale. In sidings I have used very fine dust rather than ballast – the key is to look at photographs to seen what the prototype was like and try to capture the same appearance, remembering that there were changes over the years and there was a difference in practice between various companies in both method and materials.

Distance and clearances

The distance between adjacent tracks is measured between the outside edges of the railheads. On curves the space must be wider than on the straight to allow for the 'overthrow' of vehicles unless the standard space is wide enough to give a safe clearance between vehicles. When working to scale or very close to scale modelling standards, little or no compromise is necessary, but with some modelling standards considerable adjustments have to be made. In order to show what the various clearances were on the prototype I have included a table of dimensions taken from the textbook *Railway Permanent Way*, to enable modellers to make their own calculations.

Above: This delightful view of a double-track main line was taken in 1910 and shows the Midland line in the Hope Valley. Note the accommodation crossing to the left of the picture. I have included this view to complement the accompanying drawings and perhaps inspire modellers to include this type of landscape in a layout. *Author's collection*

Right: This undated but probably *c*1900 picture of the North Staffordshire station at Kidsgrove Junction (Harecastle) has been included to illustrate the practice of 'boxing up' the ballast so that it covered the sleepers. Other points to note are the barrow crossing between the platforms and the narrow foot crossing in the foreground, together with the checkrail on the curve to the left. Modellers frequently have to use sharp curves, so may be there is a case for including checkrails even if they are not required to keep the stock on the rails! On the full-size railway checkrails are required on passenger lines (Ministry of Transport Blue Book) at 10 chains or less, but railway custom was to fit them on both goods and passenger lines with curves sharper than 12 chains. As Martin Welch remarks, PW men did not like ballasting up to rail level, thus hiding the sleepers; repairing track faults became much more of a task, defects would be hidden from view, and lifting and packing became a nightmare. Ballast above sleeper level performs no function other than providing pathways or roadways for road vehicles. *British Railways*

SPACES (clear).	Usual.	.... Ry.
	ft. ins.	
Standard between a pair (Up and Down) of Main Tracks........	6 0 *	
Between a pair of Main Tracks and one or a pair of additional Running Tracks	10 0 *	
Between a Running Track and a Siding	10 0	
Between a Running Track and a Catch Siding....................	6 0	
Between Goods Yard Sidings......	6 0	
Between Goods Yard Sidings, for Cartways	24 0	
Between Coal Sidings	6 0	
Between Marshalling or Sorting Sidings	7 0	
Between Carriage Sidings	8 0	
Space to allow for Lamp Posts between Sidings, etc.	8 0 to 10 0	
Space to allow for Large Main Line Signal Post	10 6 to 11 0	
Space to allow for Ordinary Main Line Signal Post	10 0	
Space for Siding Signal Post	9 8	

* Board of Trade Requirements.

	Usual.	.............Rly.
Absolute minimum clearance to structures above platform height, on passenger lines...	4' 6"	
Desirable ditto. ...	5' 0" to 7' 0"	
Minimum clearance to structures in Goods Yards, such as to sides of Warehouse doorways	4' 3"	
Desirable ditto ...	4' 6" to 7' 0"	
On curves add to above the versed sine on a chord of ...	40 ft.	
To the inside of curves add the super-elevation multiplied by	2	
Add for oscillation on curves ...	1"	

Left and above: These dimensions, which generally applied to all British railway companies, are taken from *Railway Permanent Way*, and can be used by modellers to calculate the various clearances that applied.

Below: This scene on Woden Road, an 0 gauge model of a typical West Midlands branch terminus, was built by members of the Wolverhampton Model Railway Club. Eric Harrison, who together with the late Geoff Powell constructed the signals while the signal box was the work of Cliff Bate, built the distinctive GWR Railcar. *Tony Wright, courtesy British Railway Modelling*

Modellers will encounter certain terms that require explanation. An example is **Fouling point**, which is the point at which the space between two converging tracks becomes insufficient to allow vehicles on them to safely clear each other. To further complicate matters, the fouling point for running or passenger tracks was taken where the space was 6 feet, but in goods sidings the fouling point was often taken at 5 feet.

The minimum horizontal distance between the outer edge of a rail and a structure or object of any kind other than a passenger platform was 2ft 4in between 3 feet above rail level and the top of a carriage door, and in order to allow space for a man to stand between a structure and an open carriage door the clearance should be about 5ft 6in.

Although not part of trackwork, the **Loading gauge** should perhaps be mentioned. The usual width of the British loading gauge was 9 feet, although all of the 'Big Four' British companies had lines that allowed a 9ft 6in width, with the GWR permitting 9ft 8in on certain lines. Heights also varied: the normal English maximum height was 13ft 9in, but the old Great Eastern allowed only 13 feet. The height was less in Scotland, with the Highland being the lowest at 12ft 9¾in.

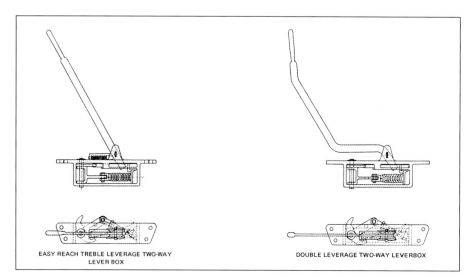

EASY REACH TREBLE LEVERAGE TWO-WAY
LEVER BOX

DOUBLE LEVERAGE TWO-WAY LEVERBOX

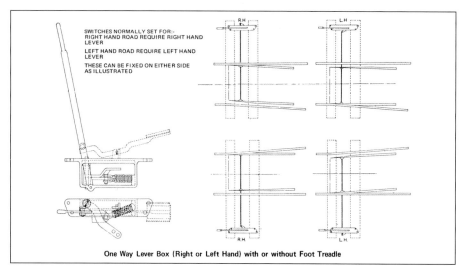

SWITCHES NORMALLY SET FOR:-
RIGHT HAND ROAD REQUIRE RIGHT HAND
LEVER

LEFT HAND ROAD REQUIRE LEFT HAND
LEVER

THESE CAN BE FIXED ON EITHER SIDE
AS ILLUSTRATED

One Way Lever Box (Right or Left Hand) with or without Foot Treadle

This picture, taken at Harpenden, shows the arrangement of a hand point lever similar to those shown in the accompanying drawings. *M. S. Cross*

Although this is an example of an early design of hand point lever, it was still in use during the 1950s. *M. S. Cross*

Left: Hand or ground point levers came in many shapes and sizes and were used to change points that were not worked from a signal box or lever frame. This drawing shows two different designs for the handle. In certain circumstances, for example in paved areas, the handle was designed to be flush with the ground. *Taff Wagon Engineering Co Ltd*

Below left: This hand point lever was designed to lay in one direction and could only be set for the other route by being held over. To assist the man operating the point a foot treadle was often used. *Taff Wagon Engineering Co Ltd*

Gradients

Most modellers try to ensure that their layouts are flat, and some will go to extraordinary lengths to ensure that there is no gradient whatsoever. I have come to the conclusion that a gradient adds immensely to the overall realism, although I admit that it can cause problems. In British practice a gradient, which is the rate at which the surface of a railway or road ascends or descends in a given length, is described as '1 in XXX'. For example, 1 in 150 means that there is a difference in level of one vertical unit in the horizontal distance of 150 units. Some years ago the practice of describing gradients as percentages was adopted, which I personally find confusing.

Point crossings, or 'frogs'

When the fixed rail that forms the lead from the switch – the 'curved closer rail' – intersects with the diverging rail there must be a free space for the wheel flanges to pass through. The British term is a 'crossing' or 'point crossing', but the common term used by modellers is 'frog'. This is an American expression, and I have never understood how or why it is used in preference to the word 'crossing', which seems to me to be more precise. However, it will come as no surprise to readers to hear that the term was also used by the GWR.

While the wheels on one side of the vehicle are passing through the crossing, the opposite wheels are travelling on a fixed rail, as on a plain piece of road, and are prevented from miscarrying by the checkrail. An ordinary crossing was shown in drawing (centre) on page 16, and a variation, whereby a solid cast steel crossing was used, was also shown.

Hand point levers

Points were usually worked by rodding from signal boxes or ground frames, and we will examine this aspect in Chapter 4. However, they could also be worked independently by a lever close to the point, and this type of point is known as a hand or ground point. Some hand point levers included a foot treadle, on which the operator stood when pulling the lever, but the majority did not include this feature. The accompanying drawings provide some examples of the different arrangements that were used.

The switch tongue rails were attached to a stretcher bar and this was connected to the operating rod. Stretcher bars varied in design, but typical examples are shown in the drawings on this page.

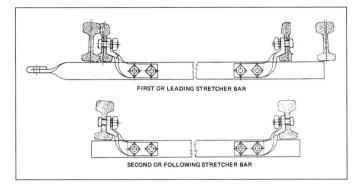

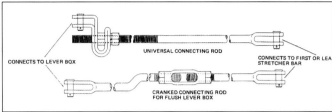

Left and above: Although most modellers use simplified arrangements for stretcher bars, I thought I ought to include drawings to show both the leading and second bars, together with an example of connecting rods. *Taff Wagon Engineering Co Ltd*

Trap and catch points

In many Board of Trade inspection reports, trap points or catch points are described as 'safety points', and they were provided on goods and mineral lines and sidings at their junction with passenger lines. They were also provided on gradients to derail a vehicle running backwards and thus prevent collision with a following train; such a 'breakaway' might be caused by a defective coupling or a snatch when the train reached the summit.

The terms are often used in the wrong context, and I think of the words of one of my drivers, who, when asked by me to explain the difference between them, said, 'Catch points catch you if you run back and trap points put you on the floor if you run too far forward.' Not the most technical of descriptions, but one that has remained in my memory since about 1949. These points are frequently ignored by modellers and I find that their presence or absence tells me much about the authenticity of a layout.

Some safety points only had one switch rail, but the majority had two and were similar to the switch rails of a point. The short length of rail leading from the trap point might go nowhere, intended just to derail the vehicle, or it might lead to a siding, some of which were very short and were often known as 'blind sidings'. Safety points could also be found in other locations, and they will be examined further in Chapter 3.

Barrow crossings

Although strictly speaking not part of the permanent way, I felt that barrow crossings should be included here. At stations with more than one platform it was necessary to move passengers' luggage and parcels from one to another. This might be done by a subway or a lift and bridge over the track, or on the level via a barrow crossing, generally but not always under the watchful eye of the signalman. I have never found any document that specified the required dimensions, but since they were usually made from re-used sleepers they would be either 9 feet or 8ft 6in wide; where space was restricted they would be not less than 6 feet wide. Foot crossings were similar but they were usually only about 2 to 3 feet wide. Illustrations are found in this chapter and Chapter 3.

Right: This picture, taken at London Road Junction, Derby, shows a single-bladed catch point protecting the running lines. In addition we can also see an example of a loading gauge and barrow crossing. *M. S. Cross*

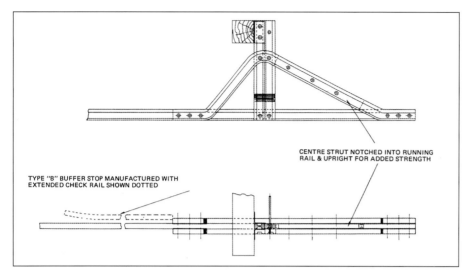

TYPE "B" BUFFER STOP MANUFACTURED WITH
EXTENDED CHECK RAIL SHOWN DOTTED

CENTRE STRUT NOTCHED INTO RUNNING
RAIL & UPRIGHT FOR ADDED STRENGTH

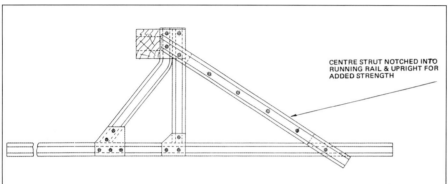

CENTRE STRUT NOTCHED INTO
RUNNING RAIL & UPRIGHT FOR
ADDED STRENGTH

Buffer stops and scotch blocks

There can be few layouts that do not require a buffer stop, or, as many railwaymen called them, 'stop blocks'. The usual width of a buffer beam was 7ft 6in and the height above rail level of the centre of the beam was 3ft 6in. The pre-Grouping companies often had distinctive designs, and an article in *Midland Record* No 7 records details of Midland Railway practice, but of course these and the many other distinctive designs used by British companies were still in service up to the end of steam and beyond. To add to the information already in print, I have included some typical designs that were installed on British railways both before and after nationalisation. In addition to the normal type of rail-built buffer stop, they were also constructed from timber, usually old sleepers, or formed part of a loading dock or the end of a bay platform.

Left and above right: These drawings show four modern arrangements for buffer stops. Both before and after the Grouping there were distinctive company designs that remained in service for many years, so a pre-Grouping design would not be out of place on a model of the British Railways era. A buffer stop in a platform had to carry a red light at night – nowadays it carries three. Although when it was on a platform line the face of the buffer plank was painted red, I have found nothing else about painting requirements for buffer stops. Therefore it is safe to assume that the steel rail was exposed to the elements and took on a rusty colour. On the other hand, the timber work was probably treated with creosote. *Taff Wagon Engineering Co Ltd*

Left: In addition to being built from rails, buffer stops could also be made from sleepers. Although such structures differed in size and style, the general design was similar to this example photographed at Harvington in the 1950s.
M. S. Cross

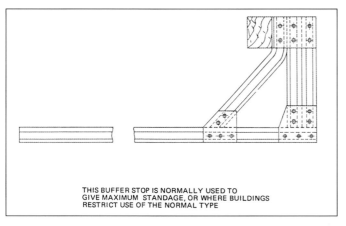

THIS BUFFER STOP IS NORMALLY USED TO
GIVE MAXIMUM STANDAGE, OR WHERE BUILDINGS
RESTRICT USE OF THE NORMAL TYPE

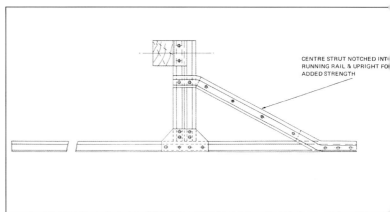

CENTRE STRUT NOTCHED INT·
RUNNING RAIL & UPRIGHT FO·
ADDED STRENGTH

Above: This photograph of the buffer stops at Windermere Lakeside station, taken on 29 April 1965, illustrates a number of features that may appeal to modellers. The construction of the buffer stops with the rails continuing into the end wall was a common arrangement. Note also the hand point lever, presumably operating a crossover between the two platform lines to enable a locomotive to run round its train; presumably also the crossover was bolt-locked at the signal box, and when the levers were released they would probably be operated by the locomotive fireman. A rather nice touch is the wrought iron fence at the end of the platform. *Author's collection*

Above: Buffer stops of pre-Grouping origin remained in service until the end of steam and beyond, and displayed many detail differences. Here we see an example of a former NER buffer stop, photographed in 1967. *W. O. Steel*

Below left: An example of a buffer stop in Scotland, at Wormit in 1967. *W. O. Steel*

Below: This picture was taken at Ascot on 1 June 1967. These photographs demonstrate that the design of buffer stops was quite distinctive, and modellers should try to ensure that their examples are correct for the area being reproduced on their layouts. *W. O. Steel*

Buffer stops were not the only way of preventing rolling-stock from moving too far along a siding. To stop a vehicle running out of a siding a 'scotch block' might be used, or a 'wheelstop', sometimes called a 'stop block'. Wheelstops were often used at the end of roads in engine sheds, and elsewhere when space was limited and traffic speed low.

Water troughs

I have never seen a model incorporating water troughs, and little of value to modellers appears to have been written about them. They would be rather difficult to model, so other than to record they were a feature on some, but not all, railway companies, they are not included in this book.

Right: I have never found any written explanation as to why scotch blocks were used instead of catch points – possibly where space was a major consideration, and they were also less expensive. I have included this drawing of a Midland Railway example, and no doubt the design varied slightly from company to company, but the principle was the same, to stop vehicles moving on to running lines.

Below left: Turntables to turn wagons at goods stations remained in service until the end of steam, but the use of turntables to turn carriages ceased when the vehicles became too long to be shunted by this method. Although this picture, taken at Hereford during the Victorian era, shows a wagon turntable, it is included to show the use of scotch blocks to protect the passenger lines from any unauthorised movement by a wagon. This arrangement remained in use on British railways for many years, but latterly was generally at goods stations rather than protecting passenger lines. *Hereford City Library*

Below right: Wheelstops were permanently fixed to the rail and were used in engine sheds to prevent engines from running off the end of the shed roads. They were also found in many goods stations and were usually arranged so that they could be lowered in order to allow wagons to pass them. This drawing shows how they were constructed. *Taff Wagon Engineering Co Ltd*

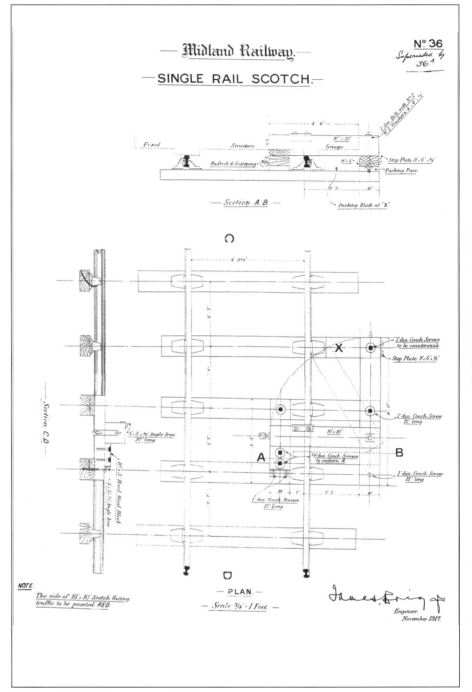

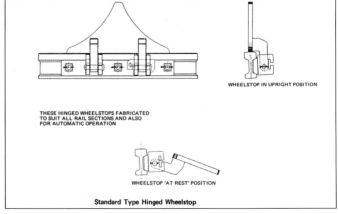

Right: Llwymawr is a model of a typical GWR Cambrian section station that has been built to P4 standards by Rex Ashton. The signals and signal box are made from Ratio parts and together with the distinctive coaches represent make a delightful county branch line. *Tony Wright, courtesy British Railway Modelling*

Glossary of trackwork terms

Simple curve	A line that is a portion of the circumference of a circle, ie the arc of a circle.
Contra-flexure	Two connected curves that bend in opposite directions.
Similar flexure	Two connected curves that bend in the same direction.
Tangent	In geometry, a straight line touching but not cutting a curve.
Tangent point or Springing of curve	The point from which a curve springs, ie where it touches a line or other curve, the two being said to be 'tangential' at that point.
Compound curve	A curve formed by two or more simple curves tangential to each other and of similar flexure.
Reverse curve	A curve formed by two simple curves tangential to each other but of opposite flexure.
Transition curve	A curve making a gradual change from a straight line to a simple curve or from one curve to another.
Gauge	The least distance between the railheads of track where they are touched by the flanges of the wheels.
Up and down lines	A means of identifying the direction of running lines. Generally lines carrying trains from London are down lines and those carrying traffic to London are up lines. Similarly, with railways whose headquarters were not in London, the line from the town or city where the main offices were located was the down line; for example, the Midland line from Derby to Bristol was down and from Bristol to Derby was up. On single lines used by trains travelling in both directions the terms up and down described the direction of the train movement.
Goods line	A line that was not passed or signalled for use by passenger trains.
Fouling point	The point at which the space between two converging tracks becomes insufficient to allow vehicles on them to clear each other safely.
Clearance	The horizontal distance from the outer edge of a rail to a structure or object of any kind.
Headway	The height from rail level, ie the top of the rail, to the underside of a structure over the track.
Loading gauge	The outline with respect to a base line across the top of the rails beyond which no part of a vehicle or its load may project.
Flying junction	A junction where, for example, a down branch line gains the down main line by crossing the up main line on a bridge, to avoid the two lines crossing on the level.
Burrowing junction	As above, but where the branch line passes beneath the main line.
Loop	A track connected to the same main line at both ends, used to relieve the main line. Loops maybe classified as Passenger running loops, Goods running loops, or Refuge loops. Goods, but not Passenger, loops must be provided with safety points, although at certain places both the Board of Trade and the Ministry of Transport may have required them.
Refuge siding, Lay-by, Lie-by, Pass-by or Relief siding	Different terms for a siding used for the reception of trains, usually goods, while other trains pass by on the main line. They have trailing connections from the main line and are used to enable a slow-moving train to be overtaken by a following faster train.
Catch or runaway points	Trailing switches inserted in a main line to derail vehicles accidentally running back down an incline. They are normally positioned at least a maximum train length for the line to the rear of a stop signal on a gradient of 1 in 250 or steeper.
Safety or trap points and sidings	Board of Trade rules state that 'safety points' must be provided on goods lines and sidings at their junctions with passenger lines. Where there is sufficient space the safety points might lead into a safety siding otherwise named a 'trap', 'runaway', 'catch siding', 'sand drag' (see below) or 'blind siding'.
Buffer stop or buffer block	A structure designed to stop vehicles that come into contact with it.
Stop block or wheelstop	Blocks designed to stop vehicles by contact with their wheels; usually fixed, but some were moveable.
Scotch block	A pivoted or hinged block that can be placed across a rail to prevent vehicles passing a certain point.
Sand drag	A layer of sand on the top of a rails beyond a trap point to bring a vehicle or train gradually to a stand.
Derailer	A block that may be moved on to the rail by a lever worked by a signalman or from a ground frame to derail vehicles attempting to pass without authority.
Chain drag	A hook attached to a heavy chain arranged so as to catch the axle of a moving wagon and so bring it to a stand.
Facing points	Points on a running road used to divert trains travelling in their normal direction.
Trailing points	Points on running lines other than facing points.

Chapter Two

Historical Review of the Development of Signalling

This chapter aims to provide an overview of signalling from the earliest days of railways until the end of the steam era, although many of the colour light signals described will be familiar to modellers of the post-1968 period. Space considerations will allow no more than a 'broad brush' treatment, and I have decided to concentrate on the principles of signalling, which were common to all British railway companies, and to show some detail variations, inviting readers to refer to the sources given in Appendix 2 for further information. There will also be references to 'train working', which could have been included in the next chapter, but I felt that by blending the subject of signals with how and when they were used might provide a better understanding of the subject.

The early days of the British railway system are fascinating. Unfortunately they predated photography and contemporary accounts are limited. As far as modellers are concerned it is not a period that commands much interest, but we cannot ignore the beginning of signalling, as it forms the origins of the modern system. From the earliest years policemen were employed to protect railway property and to ensure that order was maintained with the workforce. In many respects the railways were a development of coaching practice and, accommodation apart, the railway station fulfilled the role of a traditional coaching inn. On the railway the role of the policeman was to ensure that the line was clear for the arrival of a train, and in 1838 the GWR issued instructions to its policemen and engine drivers that the signal for 'All Right' was the right hand held in a horizontal position. For 'Caution' or 'Slow Down' the arm was held straight up, and for 'Stop' both hands were held above the head. During the hours of darkness hand lamps showing different colours were used: 'All Right' was a white light, 'Caution' was a green light, and 'Stop' or 'Danger' was a red light. During daylight, as an alternative to the arm signals, white, green and red flags were also used to advise drivers. From 1841 the railways began to use 'exploding signals', better known

Below left: In *Railway Operation for the Modeller*, the first book in this series, I illustrated some examples of pre-semaphore signals; one was a type of disc signal used in connection with the time-interval working on the London & Birmingham Railway, and the other was a disc-and-crossbar signal used on the Great Western Railway. Here, though, is the first semaphore signal, installed at New Cross on the Croydon Railway in 1841; soon further examples were erected on the line to Brighton. This signal displayed three aspects: as shown indicated 'Danger', inclined downward at 45 degrees was 'Caution', and when the signal was lowered into a slot in the post and could not be seen the aspect was 'Clear.' At night red, green and white lamps indicated the 'Danger', 'Caution' and 'Clear' aspects. Note that the signal has two control levers, one to move the arm and the other to rotate the lamp to show the required colour.

Below: This drawing is dated 1875 and provides an example of Midland Railway practice at that time. Note that the semaphore arm, when lowered to show the 'Clear' aspect, was hidden in a slot in the post, and that in order to conceal the arm the post was wider at the top. Unfortunately the drawing does not show how the signal was operated, but it was almost certainly by a lever at the base of the post. It was common practice at this time to mount two arms on a single post; one for up-line trains and the other for down-line trains. Although I have never seen a drawing to confirm how they were worked, I assume that if trains were travelling in opposite directions at the same time the slot was large enough to accommodate both arms.

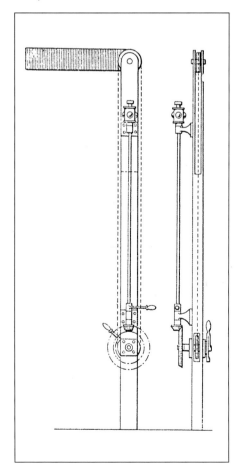

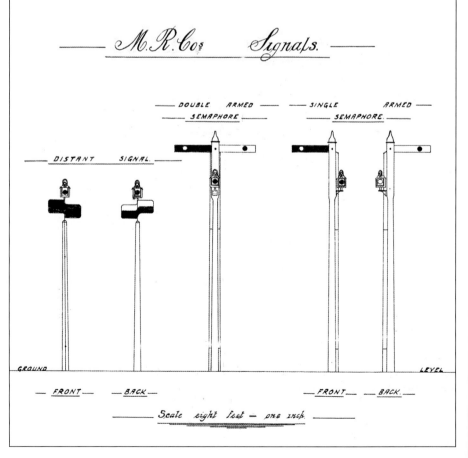

as detonators, to warn drivers, and this system continued throughout the steam era and beyond.

In the absence of fixed signals, and before the time interval system was introduced, trains were kept apart by a) working to a fixed timetable and running to time or to a sequence, b) policemen at stations controlling the movements, c) drivers keeping a sharp look-out, and d) guards protecting their trains from rear-end collisions should the need arise. As the level of traffic and speeds increased, this method of working could not continue, and the first development was the introduction of the fixed signal, ie a signal attached to a post permanently fixed in the ground; the signal was worked by a lever at the base of the post. The first fixed signals provided a variety of indications before the conventional semaphore signal was introduced. Some of the first signals were red or white lights placed on the top of the signal post. Others were in the form of a board, with D-shaped and circular boards probably the most common shapes. These boards were attached to a spindle and turned by a man standing at the base of the post. When the board was end-on it signified 'All Right', but when the driver saw the face of the board he knew that it was a 'Danger' signal. This end-on position was not really a signal, since the board could not be seen, and the absence of a clear signal could lead to misunderstandings between the driver and 'signalman'. This ultimately led to the adoption of a system of signalling used by the Army and known as semaphore signalling.

The first recorded use of a semaphore signal was in 1841 at New Cross on the Croydon Railway, when a three-position signal was erected. When the arm was horizontal it indicated 'Danger', a 45-degree downward inclination was 'Caution', and when the arm was lowered straight down and concealed in a slot in the signal post it signified 'All Right' or 'Line Clear'. Although the use of slotted signals found favour with some companies, others would not use them, generally on the grounds that snow could block the slot in the post.

The next development was a separate signal to give the 'Caution' aspect; thus the need for three-position signals ceased, and they were replaced by two-position signals. With the latter the horizontal arm indicated 'Stop' and when the arm was lowered it indicated that a driver could run past it; this aspect was generally known as 'Go' or 'All Right'. As we have seen in previous books in this series, the GWR was often different from the other British companies, so it will come as no surprise to learn that this company and the LSWR were the last major companies to adopt semaphore signalling.

Although fixed semaphore signals were a great improvement, the problem of efficient working remained unresolved. Both points and signals were worked by a man pulling a lever, generally on the ground for points, or at the base of the post for signals. The solution was to group together the levers working the various signals and points in order to avoid the policeman – or signalman, as he became known – from having to run from one signal to another in order to change the indication. At first a small platform open to the elements was used, but soon the first signal cabins, or signal boxes as they became known, came into service. This enabled savings to be made and the services of pointsmen to be dispensed with.

Above: This picture of Gargrave station includes an example of a slotted-arm signal, similar to that shown in the accompanying drawing. It shows the arrangement of the ladder to enable the lampman to service the signal lamp, and we can see that the arm is operated by a lever at the base of the post. It is difficult to date this picture with certainty, but the early 1870s seems reasonable. *Hulton Picture Library*

Interlocking of signals to prevent conflicting 'Clear' indications being given to drivers dates from the 1840s when the first interlocking arrangement was installed at Bricklayers Arms, but many years were to pass before all points and signals on the British railway system were fully interlocked. Reading the reports of the Board of Trade Inspectors and the defensive arguments of railway company directors and senior managers, it is clear that the added expense of interlocking was often far from welcome and considered to be unnecessary.

The final stage, the interlocking of points with the signals relating to them, so that no conflicting movement could take place, was still in the future as the pros and cons were debated. It took an accident at Armagh in 1889 to change opinions, and this led to the Regulation of Railways Act 1889, which required universal interlocking of points and signals and the elimination of the time interval system. I suppose it could be said that many modellers work to the equivalent of pre-1889 prototype practice, a theme that we will explore in Chapter 5.

Above: This photograph of Sutton Coldfield station in about 1862-63 shows how early signals and points were worked before they were connected to signal boxes. Although the photographer's attention is directed towards the LNWR passenger train, my interest is the signal. The large lever works a set of points – at first points were worked by a wire, in a similar manner to signals, rather than by rods. The small lever on the post controls the signal arm, which unfortunately cannot be seen on this print; however, the same picture was reproduced in *Steaming up to Sutton* and shows a signal with a separate lamp and a spectacle that appears to move in front of the lamp. What is curious is that the signal arm is either unpainted or painted in a fairly light grey. This picture is particularly important because it is one of the earliest showing semaphore signalling. *Author's collection*

Having mentioned the time interval system (which we will consider further in Chapter 3), there is a need to place it within the chronological sequence of the story of signalling development. In simple terms, it was the practice of working to a fixed timetable and ensuring that trains were separated by time rather than space (the latter being the principle employed by the later 'block' system). By ensuring that trains were not allowed to follow each other too closely, and requiring the driver to ensure that he did not catch up with the preceding train, all that was required was a policeman with a timetable that told him when trains would arrive and depart and a watch or sand-glass timer. The fixed signals were for the protection of trains approaching the station, generally from the rear. At first there was no method of communicating between stations, but this came with the advent of the telegraph.

When there were comparatively few trains the time interval system was a reasonably safe method of working. The problem arose when trains broke down between stations, in particular during the night or in snow or foggy conditions. It should also be remembered that many years were to pass before a good braking system for passenger trains became available, so stopping a train in an emergency was not easy for the driver, even with the assistance of the guard or guards (if there was more than one) and the brakesmen. As far as freight trains were concerned, the British railway system continued to run the majority of trains using wagons having only hand brakes, and it was not until well after the end of steam that automatically braked freight trains were in universal use on the British railway system.

Thus the system of a policeman stopping trains at stations with his red flag or red light, or by the use of a fixed signal showing a 'Danger' indication, was the normal practice during the early days of our railway history.

If there was a train standing at a station, having perhaps been delayed for some reason, the driver of an approaching train would have no knowledge of the state of affairs ahead. This problem was solved by the introduction of the Distant signal, or, as it was also known, the Distance or Auxiliary signal. Whereas many fixed signals were worked by pulling a lever at the base of the post, Distant signals were worked by the signalman pulling a lever that was connected to a wire that ran to the signal; thus Distant signals were worked from a concentration point, or, as it became, a signal box. When I was on the footplate it was impressed upon me that the Distant was the most important of all signals because it told the driver the state of the road ahead. If it was 'on' (showing the 'Caution' aspect) we knew that the next Stop signal would almost certainly also be on, or against us, but if it was 'off' we knew that all the other Stop signals through the section ahead would be clear. The accompanying diagram on page 37 shows the relationship between the Distant and other signals.

During the early years of the Distant signal some variations in the method of working existed, but gradually it began to assume the form that most modellers will recognise. The 'fish-tail' arm appeared in 1872, being introduced by the London & South Western and London Brighton & South Coast Railways. For many years the light for a Distant signal was red for 'Caution' and green for 'Clear'. The arms were also painted red like a Stop signal. The Great Central and Great Northern Railways introduced the yellow light for Distant signals just prior to the 1923 Grouping, but it was not until 1926 and 1928 that the Great Western and the LMS respectively adopted yellow for the colour of the Distant signal arm and the light when the signal displayed 'Caution'. This revision became a requirement of the Ministry of Transport in 1928. LMS Board Minute 1924 dated 29 November 1928 authorised the expenditure of £16,332 to comply with the MoT request regarding 'alterations in colour of lights and arms of distant signals, shunting signals and calling-on arms'. There

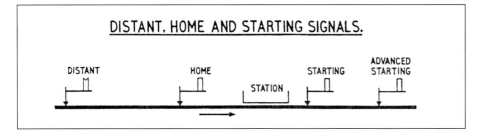

DISTANT, HOME AND STARTING SIGNALS.

Below left: Some modellers include colliery branches as part of their layouts, and this example of a colliery branch signal was photographed at Haydock, Lancashire, in May 1950. It has separate spectacles for each arm, but there is only one lamp. I assume that it was originally a railway company signal, but I have no idea of its origin. A similar slotted-post signal can be seen on page 32 of Richard Foster's book on LNWR signalling (see the References); photographed in 1933, it confirms the use of slotted signals on the LMS ten years after the Grouping. *W. S. Garth*

was also a change for calling-on arms, which were to show a white light at night. Therefore modellers with layouts set in the pre-Grouping period or during the early years of the Grouping should pay particular attention to the colour of their Distant signals.

Although I recall being told that at one time Distant signals were red, it was not until a number of years after I left railway service that I became fully aware what this meant, that at one time they looked very similar to Stop signals. At a location where the signalling was simple, this would not be too much of a problem, but at complex junctions the presence of only red and green lights could be confusing, particularly if a signal light had failed and was not exhibiting a light. An early recollection of footplate work was the feeling that I would never be able to understand or, to use a railway term, read the signals, remains with me, and I never cease to admire the old railwaymen who drove trains in all manner of weather conditions without any problems.

Another personal recollection is that from time to time I recall seeing what I would have described as 'old-fashioned signals' in service. Some were in the

Above: This simple diagram illustrates the relationship between the Distant signal and its related Stop signals on a single line with no connections to any adjacent lines. The Distant signal is 'in rear of' the Home signal and the subsequent related Stop signals, and gives the driver a warning of the condition of the Home, Starting and Advanced Starting signals controlled from the same signal box. The Distant signal may be passed at 'Caution', but that aspect instructs the driver to be prepared to stop at the next Home signal, or, should that be showing 'Clear', at the next Starting or Advanced Starting signal (the latter was not always provided, in which case next 'block section' would begin at the Starting signal. It was also possible to have an Inner Home signal, so a Distant signal could apply to a varying number of Stop signals. However, regardless of the number, the interlocking of the signal box was arranged so that the Distant signal arm could only show 'Clear' when all the Home and Starting signals had been pulled off and the line was clear through the block section to the first Home signal of the section in advance.

Below centre: Again, I have no idea of the origin of this signal, photographed in September 1948 but removed by May 1950. The picture was take on a colliery branch near Earlestown, Lancashire, and once more shows what could be found on colliery branches during the early years of British Railways. Note the absence of a lamp or spectacle. *W. S. Garth*

Below right: Crossbar signals of this type were in use on lines of the old Midland Railway as late as the British Railways period. I am unsure how widespread this type of signal was and which other companies used them, but banner-type signals were used at level crossings and as such come into the 'non-semaphore' category. This example was photographed in 1954 at Lamport Ironstone Sidings on the former LNWR Northampton-Market Harborough line. *John Edgington*

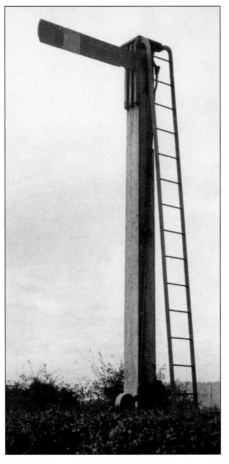

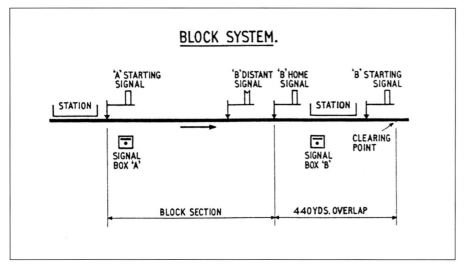

BLOCK SYSTEM.

Above: A simple block section between two signal boxes, 'A' and 'B'. Block instruments are provided in each signal box in order to provide similar indications to both signalmen simultaneously. By operating the key or handle on his instrument the signalman at box 'B' controls the indications. Coded telegraph bell signals are transmitted between the two signal boxes to enable the signalmen to exchange messages.

The operation of the section shown in the diagram is as follows. Signalman 'A' calls attention by bell code and signalman 'B' acknowledges receipt of the call. Signalman 'A' then sends him the message 'Is Line Clear for …?', the bell code identifying the class of train being offered. If the line is clear the signalman at 'B' acknowledges the signal and turns the key or handle on his block instrument, which causes the 'Line Clear' indication to be displayed on the instruments in both signal boxes. Signalman 'A' is then free to reverse his Starting signal lever, which allows the train to enter the section. As it moves into the section the signalman at 'A' sends 'Train Entering Section' to signalman 'B', who acknowledges it and places the block indicators at the 'Train on Line' position.

Although not shown on the drawing we will assume that there is another signal box, 'C', in advance of 'B'. As soon as 'B' has acknowledged the 'Train Entering Section' signal from signalman 'A', he sends the 'Call Attention' signal by bell code to signalman 'C' and the same procedure is followed. As soon as permission to enter the section is received from signalman 'C', 'B' can set his Starting signal to clear, and as soon as the train is 440 yards beyond his Home signal and has passed the Starting signal at 'B', the signalman must place his signals at 'Danger', set the block instruments in the normal position and send the 'Train out of Section' signal to signal box 'A'.

Variations are possible. For example, signalman 'B' could offer the train to signalman 'C' as soon as or even before he accepts it from 'A'; much would depend upon the circumstances, the distance between the signal boxes, and the class and speed of the train. An express train passing signal boxes located close together might be 'offered forward' by 'B' almost as soon as it was offered by 'A'.

Burton upon Trent area, and others at Gloucester and elsewhere. At the time I did not take too great an interest in them, but it does demonstrate that many signals were long-lived and that modellers of the early British Railways era should recognise that pre-Grouping equipment remained in service and that maybe they should feature some items on their layouts, in particular if their model is a branch line or colliery line. Some examples are seen in the accompanying photographs.

Although these early methods of train control and signalling may be considered primitive, by and large they worked and in the absence of a method of communication between stations the time interval was the most practical method available. With the invention of the electric telegraph the method of control was changed, and trains could be separated by space rather than time; thus the object of Absolute Block signalling may be defined as to prevent more than one train being in a block section between two signal boxes on the same line at the same time. A block section is defined as the portion of line between the most advanced Stop signal of one signal box and the outermost Stop signal controlled by the next. The accompanying diagram illustrates this, as well as the 'station limits', a term that we will encounter again in Chapter 3.

Although block signalling (or space interval signalling, as it was originally called) was possible from about 1850, it was to take many years before it was in universal use on passenger lines. It was made compulsory by the 1889 Regulation of Railways Act, which served to ensure that those lines still worked on the time interval system were altered within a short

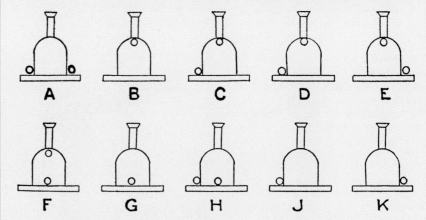

BRITISH STANDARD HEAD LIGHT INDICATIONS.

A   Express Passenger train, Breakdown Van train going to clear the line, or Light Engine going to assist disabled train.

B   Ordinary Passenger train, or Breakdown Van train not going to clear the line.

C   Fish, Meat, Fruit, Horse, Cattle, or Perishable train composed of Coaching Stock. Also Goods, Mineral and Ballast trains composed entirely of Vacuum Stock.

D   Empty Coaching Stock train.

E   Fish, Meat, or Fruit train composed of Goods Stock, Express Cattle, or Express Goods train, Class A.

F   Express Cattle or Express Goods train, Class B.
These Head Lights may also be carried by full train loads of Ballast or other materials for engineering purposes if running intact long distances.

G   Light Engine or Light Engines coupled together, or Engine and Brake.

H   Goods, Mineral, or Ballast train carrying through load to destination.

J   Through Goods, Mineral, or Ballast train stopping at intermediate stations.

K   Ordinary Goods or Mineral train stopping at intermediate stations.

As in the case of the old standard code, several railways maintain their own head light indications, especially where elaborate systems to show destinations and routes are employed. In some instances special codes are used in the London area, the standard code applying elsewhere. On certain lines discs are used by day in lamp positions; the usual practice is, however, to use unlighted lamps by day. Semaphore and other types of indicators are also in use.

period of time. The reasons for the delay in the introduction of the Absolute Block system were varied, but generally it was all about improvements costing money that the railway companies did not want to spend.

One safety requirement of the Absolute Block system was the quarter-mile overlap beyond the first Stop signal, which had to be clear before a train could be accepted. Unfortunately most modellers do not have the luxury of space – or perhaps I should say length of line – between signals, and various methods to overcome this problem are considered in Chapter 5.

By using different bell codes signalmen were able to 'talk' to each other and control the movement of trains. It was the need to identify trains approaching a signalman and to describe the trains that he was offering forward that led to the introduction of headlamp codes. In previous books in this series various examples of codes in use at different times have been featured, and it would be quite impossible to show every variation that was employed, in particular on those railways that used discs as route indicators or where discs replaced lamps. However, a further example of codes is shown in the accompanying diagram, and I have also included some examples of bell codes.

We should also consider lines that were not used for passenger trains, where a more simple system of

Left: The standard headlamp codes on Britain's railways were revised in 1918 and these codes, with a few local exceptions, remained in use until replaced by the British Railways code introduced in 1950. This in turn was superseded in 1962 by a ten-classification code. Prior to 1918 some codes required three headlamps, so a code that employed only two lamps would show a saving for the railway companies in the number of lamps required and the paraffin burned on a daily basis. Rather than use a particular railway code I have reproduced the code that was published in the 1923 *Railway Year Book*.

Right: I enjoy the use of bell codes on a model, but it is not always a good idea, in particular if the signal boxes are close to each other. However, there are way to overcome this: by using a very simple code, LEDs (light-emitting diodes) can replace the bells. Although there were slight variations between the bell codes used by the four major British railway companies, I felt that if I gave the codes of one of the 'Big Four', in this case the Great Western, it would provide a good idea of the various codes that were used.

Pages 40 & 41: This diagram is one of several from an undated and incomplete GWR document, and its value is that it shows the three-position power-operated upper-quadrant signal used by that company (so if a modeller of GWR practice wants to be different…!). In addition this double page spread also shows a variety of GWR signals and other 'signallinjg features' that could be found on all British Railways. For example, Limit of Shunt, Stop, C&T boards were used by all companies.

GREAT WESTERN RAILWAY—DOUBLE LINES

†Call attention	1
†Emergency "Call attention" signal (to precede emergency bell signals only)	A number of beats in rapid succession

Is Line Clear for :—

Express passenger train, express streamline rail car, breakdown van train going to clear the line, or light engine going to assist disabled train, or empty coaching stock train timed at express passenger speed	4
Ordinary passenger train, "mixed" train, or breakdown van train not going to clear the line	3—1
Branch passenger train	1—3
Rail motor-car, auto-train, or streamline rail car	3—1—3
Parcels, newspapers, fish, meat, fruit, milk, horse, cattle, or perishable train composed entirely of vacuum fitted stock with the vacuum pipe connected to the engine	5
Express freight, live stock, perishable, or ballast train partly vacuum fitted with not less than one-third vacuum-braked vehicles connected by vacuum pipe to engine ("C" headlamps) ...	4—4
Express freight or ballast train conveying a stipulated number of vacuum-braked vehicles connected by vacuum pipe to engine and authorised to run at a maximum speed of 35 m.p.h. ("D" headlamps)	2—2—3
Empty coaching stock train not specially authorised to carry "A" headlamps	2—2—1
Express freight, fish, meat, fruit, or cattle train, or ballast train or breakdown crane not proceeding to an accident ("E" headlamps) ...	3—2
Through fast freight train conveying through load ("F" headlamps)	1—4
Light engine or light engines coupled together or engine and brake van	2—3
Freight, mineral, or ballast train, or train of empties carrying through load to destination ("H" headlamps)	3—4—1
Freight, mineral, or ballast train stopping at intermediate stations ("J" headlamps)	3
Train conveying out of gauge or exceptional load	2—6—2
Branch freight train	1—2
Ballast train, freight train, or inspection train requiring to stop in section	1—2—2
Trolley requiring to go into or pass through tunnel	2—1—2
†Train approaching	1—2—1
†Train entering section	2
†Section clear, but station or junction blocked ...	3—5—5
†Line clear to clearing point only	2—2—2
†Engine assisting in rear of train	2—2
†Train out of section, or obstruction removed ...	2—1
Engine arrived	2—1—3
Train drawn back clear of section	3—2—3
†Obstruction danger	6
Blocking Back :—	
Inside Home Signal	2—4
Outside Home Signal	3—3
Blocking back outside home signal for train already in section	1—2—3
†Stop and examine	7
Cancelling "Is line clear" or "Train entering section" signal	3—5
†Train passed without tail lamp :—	
In advance	9
In rear	4—5
†Train divided	5—5
Shunt train for following train to pass ...	1—5—5
†Train or vehicles running away on wrong line ...	2—5—5
†Train or vehicles running away on right line ...	4—5—5
Opening of signalbox	5—5—5
Closing of signalbox	7—5—5
Testing block instruments, bells, and gongs ...	16
Time	8—5—5
Lampman or Fogsignalman required	9—5—5
Testing controlled or slotted signals	5—5—5—5
Take slot off—train waiting	3—4

The ordinary "Call Attention" signal (1 beat) must precede all signals except those marked thus †

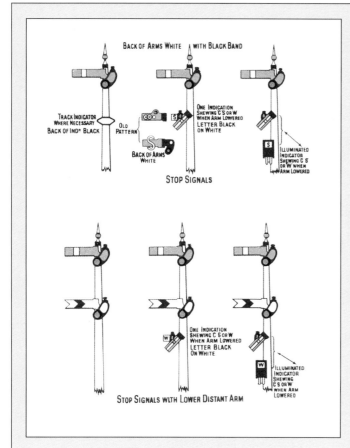

STOP SIGNALS

STOP SIGNALS WITH LOWER DISTANT ARM

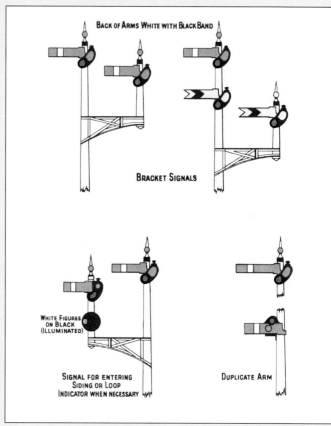

BRACKET SIGNALS

DUPLICATE ARM

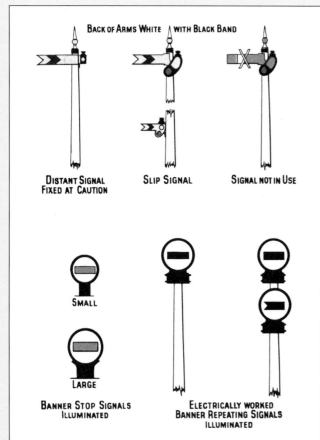

DISTANT SIGNAL FIXED AT CAUTION

SLIP SIGNAL

SIGNAL NOT IN USE

BANNER STOP SIGNALS
ILLUMINATED

ELECTRICALLY WORKED
BANNER REPEATING SIGNALS
ILLUMINATED

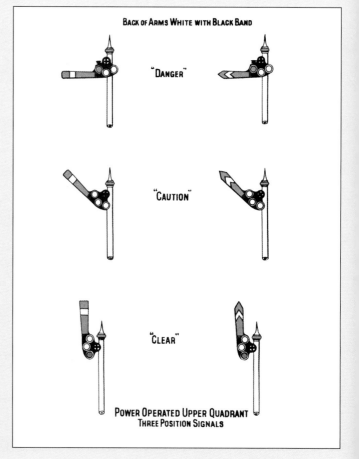

"DANGER"

"CAUTION"

"CLEAR"

POWER OPERATED UPPER QUADRANT
THREE POSITION SIGNALS

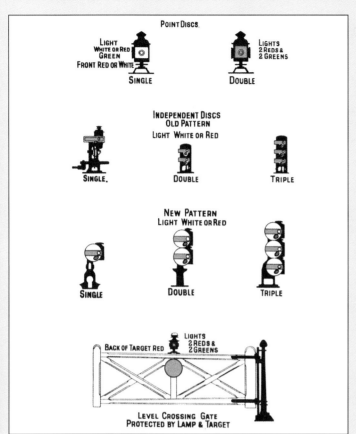

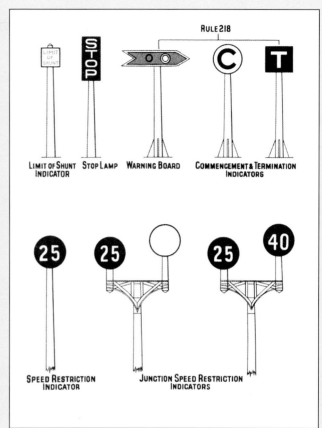

COLOUR-LIGHT SIGNALS,

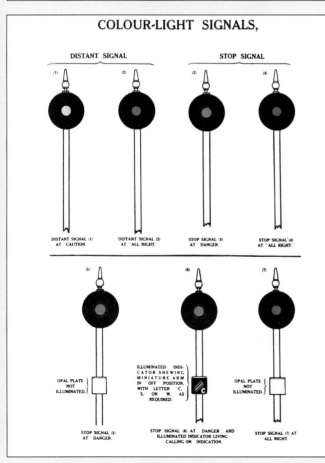

FOR RELIEF AND MAIN LINES.

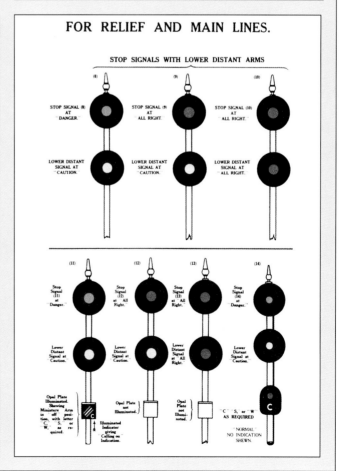

signalling was employed. The most common was the Permissive Block system, where there was no overlap beyond the Home signal in advance, and after being cautioned additional trains were allowed to enter a goods line already occupied by a train or trains. There were also often local regulations that permitted two trains on one line at large passenger stations. The use of a bell signal was employed in goods stations and marshalling yards, while the old Midland Railway telegraph bell system remained in use on the LMS. My own experiences of more than one train on a running line were largely in the Birmingham area, where it was not uncommon for there to be as many as five trains on the down goods line between Water Orton and Washwood Heath and on the up goods line between Kings Norton and Northfield. It was common practice to run up to the brake-van of the train in front, and often the train crew would join the guard in his brake-van; in bad weather conditions it was more comfortable to be in the brake than to remain on the footplate.

As we have seen, during the Victorian era three-position signals were used in conjunction with the time interval system, but following the adoption of the block system two-position signals became the normal method of advising drivers of the state of the line ahead. From 1914, starting with the GWR and the GCR, some three-position semaphore signals were tested in Great Britain. At about the same time the designs for the first colour light signals were finalised, and the question of future policy for signalling in Great Britain became the subject of debate. A committee appointed by the Ministry of Transport reported in 1921, and its recommendations favoured the colour light rather than the semaphore signal. The first daylight colour light signal installation was on the Liverpool Overhead Railway in April 1921, and a three-aspect colour light signal was installed by the LNER in 1923 on the former GCR line between Neasden and Marylebone. In 1926 the Southern Railway re-signalled the line between Holborn Viaduct and Elephant & Castle, installing four-aspect colour light signals that included two yellow lights, or 'double yellow' as it became known. This had been recommended in 1924 by the Institution of Railway Signal Engineers, together with the use of the upper-quadrant signal for two-position signals and the abandonment of three-aspect semaphore signals. With the exception of the GWR, the main-line companies adopted this recommendation in 1926.

The colour light aspects for a three-position signal showed green at the top, yellow in the middle and red at the bottom, to be near the driver's eye level. On a four-aspect signal the second yellow light was placed above the green. Some colour light signals displayed the lights horizontally. Other variations included the searchlight signal, which had only one lens with the aspects being displayed through a vane mounted on a knife-edged bearing counterweighted to ensure that a red signal showed in case of failure. From personal experience I can say that the colour light signal gave a very clear indication, very much better than a semaphore signal, in particularly during fog or falling snow. Although the colour light signal is commonplace today, most modellers of the steam era will need to use only semaphore signals on their layouts. During my days on the footplate from late

1947 until the mid-1950s colour light signals were not common, so unless you are modelling an area that was re-signalled with colour lights it is not very likely that modellers, in particular those who model branch lines, will need any, apart from possibly a Distant signal.

Running signals

The most common signals on a railway are Stop and Distant signals. The Stop signal has a square end to the arm, the Distant a 'fish-tail' end. Collectively they are known as 'running signals', as distinct from shunting or subsidiary signals. We will begin our detailed examination of the types of signals with mechanical signals, although I have also included a few early examples to show how it all began.

Running signals control the movements of trains on running lines and serve to maintain a safe distance between trains running in the same direction on the same line. They also provide directional indication at junctions where the line divides, and protection where lines converge. Usually they are to be found on the left-hand side of the line, but there were exceptions, the primary concern being to ensure good sighting for the driver. For this reason the height of the post also varied, and some examples of the variations that could be found have been included in this section.

Distant signals

These are always placed in the rear of the Home signal to which they apply. In other words, the

The first signal arms were painted in a single plain colour, but soon red on the front and white on the rear became the usual arrangement. Stripes were added to make them more distinctive to drivers. Some companies used black stripes on both sides of the arm, but generally a white strip on the front and black on the rear was most common, although the Midland Railway used a white spot on the front and a black spot on the rear. Some companies added various devices in order to distinguish selected signals, such as rings on the North London and LNWR, and bars and diamonds on other lines. In order to indicate which routes were authorised by a signal, the GWR painted lettering on the signal arm.

The shape of the signal arm could also vary, examples being 'hammerheads' on the Midland and backing signal arms with holes in them on the GWR. During the Grouping era enamelled steel signal arms were introduced. Slotted signal posts are mentioned elsewhere, but in this brief review it is worth reminding LNER modellers that examples of North Eastern Railway slotted-arm signals were in service for many years after 1923. My advice to readers who wish to study the signalling practices of their favoured companies is to see what has been published. I have listed all signalling books known to me in the References section.

Below: Upper- and lower-quadrant Distant signals.

DISTANT SIGNAL ASPECTS.

ASPECT	LOWER QUADRANT	UPPER QUADRANT
CAUTION	YELLOW LIGHT	YELLOW LIGHT
PROCEED	GREEN LIGHT	GREEN LIGHT

Above: A Distant 'sky arm' signal photographed on the Cheshire Lines Committee in 1951. Those were rather spectacular and would look rather impressive on a model. Because they cost more to erect and maintain they were only used when it was necessary to raise the signal arm to a point where the driver could see it in time to bring his train to a halt should the Stop signal in advance be at danger. A lower repeating arm was always provided because as the train approached the signal the driver would lose sight of the upper arm, but the lower arm would remain in view. *W. S. Garth*

Above right: Also on the CLC in 1951 are these 'splitting' Distant signals near Northenden; note also the Distant signal for trains travelling in the opposite direction. In the distance there is a junction where the lines divide, to the left to Stockport CLC and to the right to the old Midland Railway lines to Hazel Grove. Unusually the splitting Distants are placed on either side of the line rather than on a bracketed post. *W. S. Garth*

driver will see the Distant signal before he reaches the Home, and when the arm is horizontal the aspect displayed is 'Caution', but when the arm is lowered or raised the aspect is 'Proceed'. A driver can pass a Distant signal at 'Caution', but he must be prepared to stop at the next Home signal, even though he may find that the Home or Outer Home are 'Clear' and that he will be held at the Starting or Advanced Starting signal. The interlocking of these signals is such that until all are in the 'Clear' position the Distant signal cannot be pulled off or cleared, to use two railwaymen's terms, to show that the line is clear to the Home signal of the section in advance. In full-size practice the Distant signal had to be sited sufficiently far from the Home signal to enable the driver to bring his train to a stand from the full line speed allowed.

The importance of the main-line Distant signal cannot be overstated. During fog or falling snow each signal box had an object that, if it could not be seen by the signalman from his box, meant that

he had to 'call out the fogmen'. These were usually platelayers and they were stationed at or close to the foot of the Distant signals. When the Distant signal was at 'Caution' they ensured that a detonator was placed on the top of the rail and held there by clips. When the signal showed 'Proceed' the detonator was removed. At many locations the fogman was not at the base of the signal and because it could be dangerous to cross the line it was not unusual to have a small lever frame that placed the detonator on the top of the rail or removed it as required (an example is illustrated on page 73). The work was hazardous and unpleasant, and the men were provided with a brazier for warmth and a small hut, which was placed in the horizontal position when not in use. Fogmen were not required at colour light Distant signals or on single-line branch lines. In modelling terms those signals that, on a full-size railway, would have required a fogman should have a hut and brazier. Again, a drawing of the hut will be found on page 73, in Chapter 3.

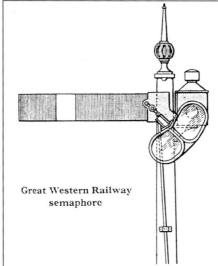

Great Western Railway
semaphore

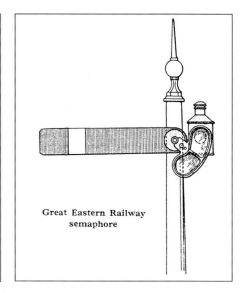

Great Eastern Railway
semaphore

Left: Although not too commonplace, the 'fixed Distant' was a Distant signal permanently fixed in the horizontal 'Caution' position. The purpose was to remind the driver to exercise caution on the approach to perhaps a junction or terminus, and they only displayed a yellow light. This example was photographed at Fenny Compton on the SMJR section in 1964. An outside contractor probably made the signal; the SMJR was a small company and would have purchased its requirements from 'the trade'. *Author's collection*

Above centre, right, below and below right: There were considerable variations in the same types of signals used by different British railway companies. Drawing A is a GWR Stop arm. Although the 'Stop' aspect – the arm in the horizontal position – was common to all railways, the amount of rise or fall varied. Great Western lower-quadrant semaphores fell to a very acute angle, which was, in my recollection, the most distinctive feature of that company's signals. On the Great Eastern (B) the fall was greater: when in the 'Clear' position they were supposed to

fall within 10 inches of the signal post. Generally the fall was around 45 degrees, although some companies preferred a greater fall to 50 or even 60 degrees. Signal arms were originally made of wood, but the LNWR introduced corrugated steel, so it seems only appropriate to show one of that company's arms here (C). The most distinctive form of semaphore signal was the 'somersault' arm as adopted by the Great Northern Railway (D). This type of signal was also used on the Taff Vale, Northern Counties and Barry railways, but did not find favour elsewhere in this country.

No doubt some readers will question how long signals of the pre-Grouping companies remained in service, and the answer is a long time! I recall visiting Chester in 1964 in order to photograph the numerous ex-LNWR signals and elsewhere examples of Midland Railway signals that were still in service after steam operation ceased in this country. No doubt other pre-Grouping companies' signals were long-lived, so under certain conditions modellers of the final years of the British steam railway could use pre-1923 signals on their layouts.

Stop signals

When the arm is horizontal it means 'Stop'. Depending upon whether it is an upper- or lower-quadrant signal, a raised or lowered arm means 'Proceed', although as we have seen 'All Right' was also used to describe a clear road aspect. 'Reversed' is another term, meaning that the lever in the signal box frame has been pulled, or reversed, and this movement has altered the aspect of the signal (this term can also apply to a lever returned to its normal position in the frame).

After 1923 the four major British companies used what were in effect standard company designs, but even so, during the 25-year life of the 'Big Four', few changes of design were made. Pre-1923 signals remained in service throughout the Grouping years and beyond 1948, while signals from the Grouping era still remain in service today. Therefore it is understandable that the signals from the pre-Grouping era represent a rich variety of design for post-1923 modellers, and as many as possible have been included in the accompanying photographs showing some variations of stop signals.

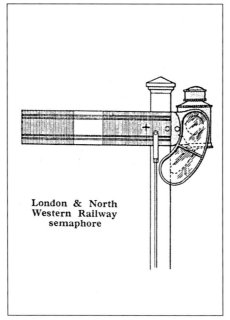

London & North
Western Railway
semaphore

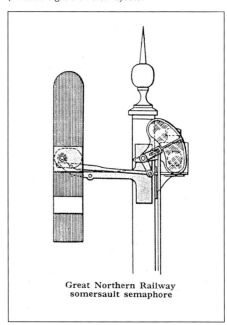

Great Northern Railway
somersault semaphore

STOP SIGNAL ASPECTS.

ASPECT	LOWER QUADRANT	UPPER QUADRANT
STOP	RED LIGHT	RED LIGHT
PROCEED	GREEN LIGHT	GREEN LIGHT

Left: Both upper- and lower-quadrant signals could be found on the British railway system although, as I have remarked before, the GWR was always different from the other major companies and did not install upper-quadrant signals.

Below: This LNER-period picture, taken at Doncaster, shows an ex-GNR somersault signal displaying the 'Clear', or 'off', aspect, to use the term with which I was familiar during my days on the footplate. *Real Photographs*

Above: I make no apologies for including this additional view of Great Northern somersault signals, as I think they are rather splendid. Note that they are 'sky arm' signals, with both the Stop and Distant signals repeated at a lower level. The signal post to the right, again with both Stop and Distant signals, is for the goods or slow line. The passenger train, hauled by GNR 4-4-2 No 278, is on the main line running under clear signals, or, as some railwaymen would say, with the 'back 'un off'. 'Back 'un' it is a railwayman's term, and when I was on the footplate Distant signals were always known by this name; later, long after I left railway service, it occurred to me that the expression had its roots in early railway history, when the Distant signal was placed back one from the Home signal. *Lens of Sutton*

Left: I have no idea where this picture was taken, but it appears to be an ex-LNWR Stop signal, which could be an outlet signal from a goods station or siding. Note the distinctive arrangement of the ladder in front of the post. *Author's collection*

Above: In November 1964, more than 40 years after the company ceased to exist, these LNWR signals were still in service at Chester. When I learned that many of the signals there were examples of pre-1923 designs, I went to photograph as many as I could. The purpose of including this picture is simply to emphasise the importance of ensuring that models reflect the varying ages of equipment in use, and that some enjoyed many years of service. *Author's collection*

Below: This drawing of a typical British 'wood bridge signal' has been included to provide information about typical dimensions and clearances. Commonly known as signal gantries, the old name is given on this 1912 drawing. *Modern Railway Working, Vol 6*

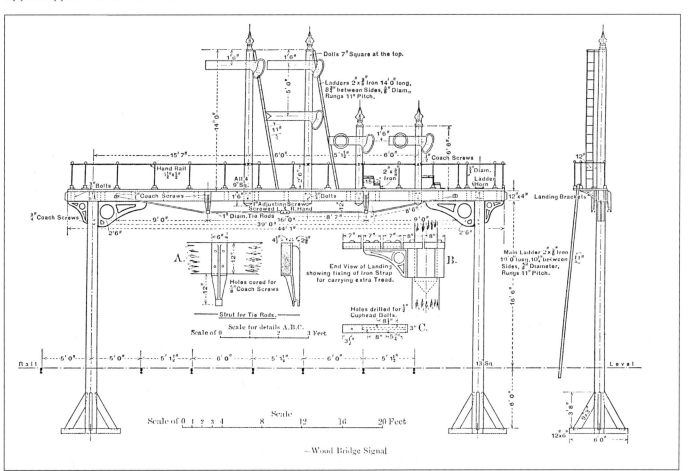

—Wood Bridge Signal

Above left: On single lines in particular, and not unknown in other locations, a single post was used to carry two signal arms, one referring to each direction of travel. This example is on the Upton-on-Severn branch of the old Midland Railway and was photographed in 1960. Note the gradient post to the right of the picture. *D. Ibbotson*

Above: After nationalisation, when the regional boundary changes meant that old railway A was now under the control of old railway B, the mixing of equipment was not unknown, and here is an example. The location is Rubery on the joint LMS/GWR Halesowen branch. Before 1948 the signalling was LMS (ex-Midland), but after nationalisation the line came under the control of the Western Region. This explains why the old Midland signal post now has a GWR arm. Modellers of the post-1948 period should be aware of this, and it was not unknown for not only signal arms but also entire signals to be replaced using the designs of the controlling Region. *D. Ibbotson*

Left: Where signal boxes were close together the Starting signal of one and the Distant signal for the next in advance were often mounted on the same post. Rather than use a picture of a conventional Stop signal over a Distant signal with both arms close together, I have included this picture of an ex-Furness Railway example, photographed in 1951 on the Bardsea branch near the Ulveston ship canal crossing. For modellers of the British Railways era it is another reminder that pre-1923 equipment was long lived. *W. S. Garth*

Right: Some semaphore signals were power-operated and this picture, taken at Southport, shows former L&YR electro-pneumatic signals. *W. S. Garth*

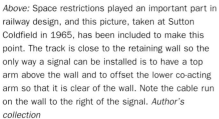

Above: Space restrictions played an important part in railway design, and this picture, taken at Sutton Coldfield in 1965, has been included to make this point. The track is close to the retaining wall so the only way a signal can be installed is to have a top arm above the wall and to offset the lower co-acting arm so that it is clear of the wall. Note the cable run on the wall to the right of the signal. *Author's collection*

Above: At some locations the driver might not get 'a clear sight of the signal', and one method used to overcome the problem was to place a sighting board behind the signal arm so that the arm could be seen against a white background. This example of a modern tubular steel post upper-quadrant stop Signal was photographed at Foxfield on the Furness section in 1965. *Author's collection*

Above: Without being aware of the track plan and signalling arrangements at Pennington station on the old LNWR, where this picture was taken in 1949, I can only draw attention to, but cannot give an explanation for, the shorter Stop and Distant arms on the left of this bracket signal. *W. S. Garth*

Left: The old-style semaphore signals were labour-intensive, and the lamps required attention on a regular basis. The rules about the procedures for cleaning and filling lamps were thorough, and the work was undertaken in a lamp room. This picture, taken at Kings Norton in 1957, shows a bracket signal with corrugated steel arms being attended to by a lampman. Also note the white diamond on the section of post that has been painted black.
R. S. Carpenter collection

Below: This north-facing view of Radford Junction has been included for three reasons. The first is to show the white diamond sign on the post, and the second is to draw attention to the ground signal with the finger pointing towards the points to which it refers. The third reason is not connected with signals, but is the barrow crossing, which connects the two platforms and is worthy of note.
H. B. Priestley

Right: I have included this picture, taken at Southport Lord Street station in 1948, to show how the top ladders were arranged to keep the lampman or fitter 'inside' the signal. This example is a splitting bracket signal with a subsidiary arm below each stop signal.
W. S. Garth

There are several types of Stop signals to consider, and we will begin with the **Home signal**. Home signals are provided to protect stations and junctions with other lines. At some locations where no Starting signal was provided the Home could also act in that capacity. The Home signal, or the Outer Home signal if more than one is provided, marks the end of the block section in the rear and the start of station limits. They are usually placed within 100 yards of a station or fouling point, although many exceptions to this rule could be found. Later practice was to place the Home signal the overlap distance (about 440 yards) from the station or the obstruction they protected.

Above: Photographed at Didsbury in 1925, this picture of the Down distant signal shows a red distant arm with a white sighting board. As explained on page 36, it was some years after the 1923 grouping that all distance signal arms were painted yellow. *D. F. Tee collection*

HOME SIGNALS.

UP HOME

STATION

UP LINE ——→

——DOWN LINE

SIGNAL BOX

DOWN HOME

Left: This diagram shows the position of the Home signals on a double line in relation to a station where there is a trailing crossover. The Home signals mark the end of the block sections and the start of station limits. At some locations Outer Home signals were provided, and these marked the point where the block section in the rear ended and station limits began.

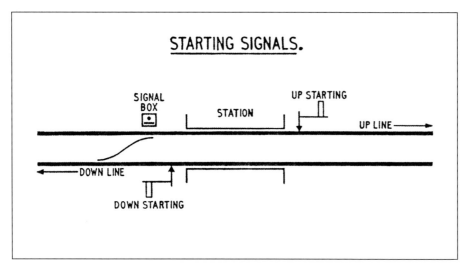

The Starting signal is also referred to as a 'Section signal', and authorises a train to enter the block section in advance. It marks the end of station limits and the start of the next block section. In many cases an Advanced Starting signal is provided, enabling shunting movements to be carried out within station limits that otherwise would have meant the train running beyond station limits and entering the block section in advance. Advanced Starting signals also allow trains to be held in a position that does not block the station or junction, which is useful if the signalman in advance cannot accept the train.

Above left: This diagram does not show the Home signals, but only the Starting signals, which, in the absence of Advanced Starting signals, mark the end of station limits and the beginning of the block sections in advance. While it would be perfectly correct not to have an Advanced Starting signal on the up line, one would have been installed on the down line, otherwise any movement over the crossover would mean the train having to be offered to the signalman in advance and accepted by him as a shunting movement. It was much easier to arrange the signals as shown in the next diagram.

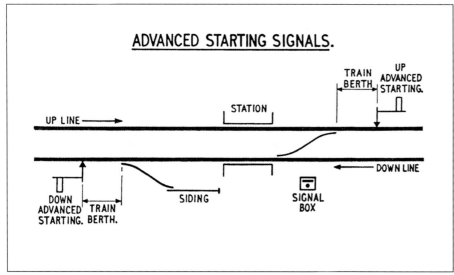

Left: This diagram shows the value of an Advanced Starting signal. A train on the down line can pass the signal box, run up to and pass the Starting signal at the end of the platform (not shown, but similar to that in the previous diagram) and set back into the down siding while still remaining within the station limits and with all the movements under the control of the local signalman. Without the Advanced Starting signal the train could only pass the Starting signal if it had been offered to and accepted by the signalman in advance. Thus the Advanced Starting signal extends the station limits and gives the signalman more flexibility.

Subsidiary signals

This class of signal controls train movements that are run at lower speeds, and they are visually different in order that they should not be confused with running signals. This type of signal can be divided into a number of categories, and it should be mentioned that numerous variations of the same type of signal existed as a result of the different railway companies creating their own designs. Generally a smaller arm, fixed below the relative Stop arm, was employed, in some cases with a form of identification as described below.

Main line to siding or running line to loop

A signal with a reduced-size arm was employed, and at night the red light for 'Stop' and the green for 'Proceed' were smaller than the lights in a running line signal.

Outlet signal from siding

Signals authorising movements from a goods line or siding where no Advanced Starting signal was provided would be a semaphore signal rather than a

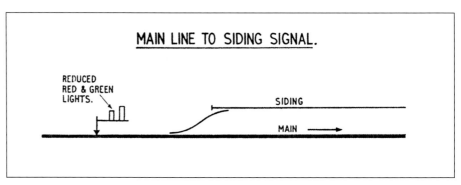

Above: This subsidiary signal authorises a train movement from the main line into the siding. (Note that the term 'siding' could indicate a single siding or lead to or from a goods station or one of the many private sidings that were of considerable size.) Track layouts and mainline connections for private sidings, collieries and railway company goods stations wwill be found in *Freight Train Operation for the Railway Modeller.*

ground signal, but generally the arm was a miniature version of a main arm on a running signal. This type of signal was also referred to as a 'tall siding signal' and could have a yellow arm to signify that it could be passed at 'Stop' for routes to which it did not apply. It

was used in goods yards when the line to which it applied was also the goods yard headshunt or shunting neck, thus allowing a train to be shunted back and forth passing the signal in the 'on' position. It would only be placed in the 'off' position when the

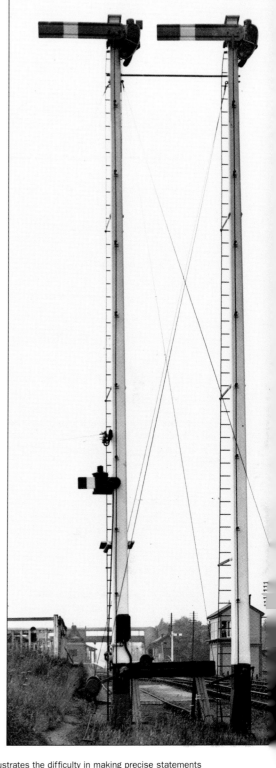

Above: A mixture of running signals – Stop and fixed Distants – with subsidiary signals. Space restrictions often meant that signal arms needed to be shorter than normal, and I have included this picture, taken at the north end of Preston in 1946, to illustrate this point. The disc signal at the base of the post is for shunt moves and has an illuminated indicator above reading 'Call on to cabin only' (the signal cabin). The very small subsidiary signal at the foot of the left-hand 'doll' (small post on a bracket or gantry) is a calling-on signal. Note also the white diamond, which indicates that the line is track-circuited and if a train is detained at this signal there is no need for the fireman to go to the signal box to remind the signalman of their presence. *W. S. Garth*

Above right: This picture illustrates the difficulty in making precise statements about signals without knowing their location; even with this information it is not easy to 'read' the signals without local knowledge. Happily, this picture appears on page 94 of Richard Foster's book on LNWR signalling (see the References), so I am able to say that it was taken in July 1916 and shows the up home signals at Cheadle Hulme. They are junction signals on two separate posts with a tie rod between them rather than the later arrangement of a bracket with two smaller posts. The right-hand arm refers to the Crewe line and the left-hand arm to the Macclesfield line. A calling-on arm is mounted low down on the left post to allow trains to draw forward on to the Macclesfield line and thus clear the line for other traffic approaching from the rear. Although the author does not say so, I assume that there was a signal to authorise a 'setting back' move from the branch, and that this shunting movement was to allow trains to be overtaken, rather than install a loop line or lie-by. *Author's collection*

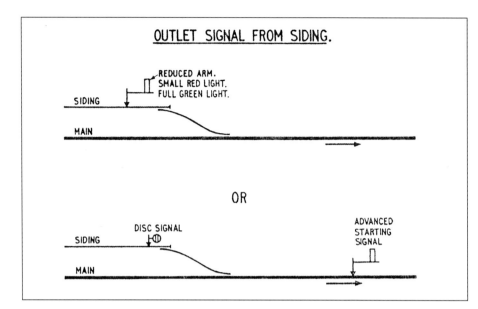

OUTLET SIGNAL FROM SIDING.

REDUCED ARM.
SMALL RED LIGHT.
FULL GREEN LIGHT.

SIDING

MAIN

OR

DISC SIGNAL

SIDING

MAIN

ADVANCED
STARTING
SIGNAL

Left: This diagram shows two alternatives for a connection from a goods siding to a running line. A disc signal would be used instead of a semaphore arm to authorise a movement from the siding to the main line when there was an Advanced Starting signal. The explanation is simple: a disc signal would not be used to authorise a train movement into the block section in advance, while a semaphore arm could give this signal. Likewise, a train stopping on the main line to attach or detach wagons would, if there was an Advanced Starting signal, still be within station limits when the movement was made, so a disc signal would be appropriate to authorise the shunting movement.

Below: This drawing, originally published in 1913 in *Modern Railway Working* Vol 6, shows a variety of different subsidiary signals, including two from the GWR.

train was leaving the yard to proceed on to the running lines.

Shunt ahead, Calling-on and Warning signals

A shunt ahead signal is located below the signal controlling the entrance to the section ahead. When lowered it allows the section signal to be passed at 'Danger', but for shunting purposes only.

In the case of a calling-on signal, the approaching train must be brought to a stand before it is lowered, and when this is done it indicates to the driver that the line between the calling-on signal and the next Stop signal is occupied. Calling-on signals are usually found at large stations where shunting movements are carried out to attach or detach vehicles to or from trains occupying the platforms, where a passenger train is running into a terminal platform with a vehicle at the stop blocks, or into a platform already occupied by a train.

Warning signals are provided for the purpose of indicating to the driver that the line is clear to the next Stop signal and that the speed of the train must be regulated accordingly. Warning signals must not be lowered until the train has been brought to a stand.

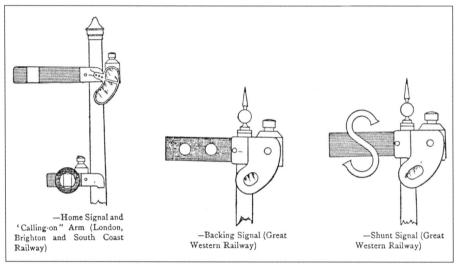

—Home Signal and 'Calling-on" Arm (London, Brighton and South Coast Railway)

—Backing Signal (Great Western Railway)

—Shunt Signal (Great Western Railway)

Below left: This is a later design of subsidiary signal, but the principle is the same and the respective functions of the indications are described in the text.

Below: It is not difficult to become confused when trying to understand the difference between warning, calling-on and shunt ahead signals, but I hope this simple drawing will assist in clarifying their functions.

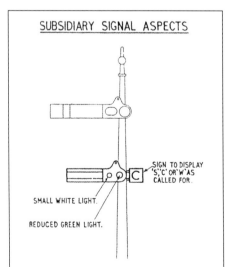

SUBSIDIARY SIGNAL ASPECTS

SIGN TO DISPLAY
'S','C' OR 'W' AS
CALLED FOR.

SMALL WHITE LIGHT.

REDUCED GREEN LIGHT.

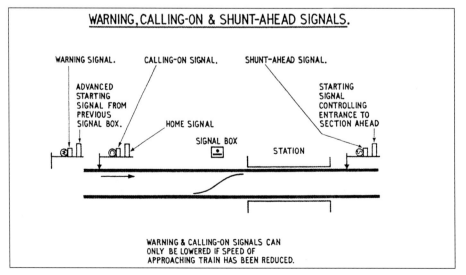

WARNING, CALLING-ON & SHUNT-AHEAD SIGNALS.

WARNING SIGNAL.

CALLING-ON SIGNAL.

SHUNT-AHEAD SIGNAL.

ADVANCED
STARTING
SIGNAL FROM
PREVIOUS
SIGNAL BOX.

HOME SIGNAL

SIGNAL BOX

STATION

STARTING
SIGNAL
CONTROLLING
ENTRANCE TO
SECTION AHEAD

WARNING & CALLING-ON SIGNALS CAN
ONLY BE LOWERED IF SPEED OF
APPROACHING TRAIN HAS BEEN REDUCED.

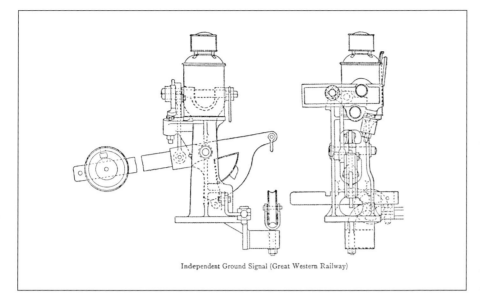

Independent Ground Signal (Great Western Railway)

Ground signals

Ground signals, often referred to as disc signals, dummies or dwarf signals, were provided for low-speed shunting movements and varied considerably in design, including discs that revolved; discs that rotated, with a horizontal red or yellow band on a white ground indicating horizontal for 'Danger' and turned for 'Proceed'; and miniature semaphore arms. Although red and green were by far the most common lights shown, some ground signals displayed a yellow light instead of red, allowing drivers to pass them for routes for which they did not apply. In some cases one ground signal could permit movement over more than one route, but at other installations there would be more than one ground signal attached vertically to the same post, each signal authorising movement over one particular route; the uppermost signal always refers to the farthest left route. According to Graham Warburton, the maximum number he recorded on a single post was five.

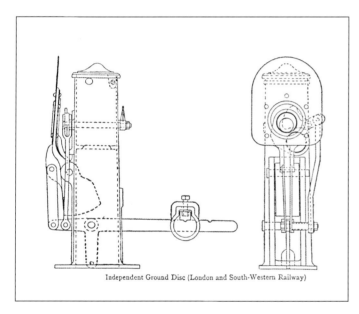

Independent Ground Disc (London and South-Western Railway)

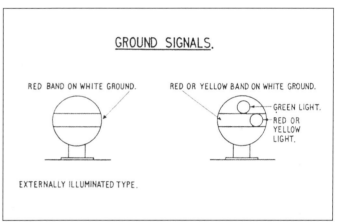

GROUND SIGNALS.

RED BAND ON WHITE GROUND.

RED OR YELLOW BAND ON WHITE GROUND.

GREEN LIGHT.
RED OR YELLOW LIGHT.

EXTERNALLY ILLUMINATED TYPE.

Ground signals have many names. Although described on the drawings as an 'Independent Ground Signal', they were also known as discs, dummies and, no doubt, other local names. The old type of revolving disc was long-lived and examples could be seen after 1948.

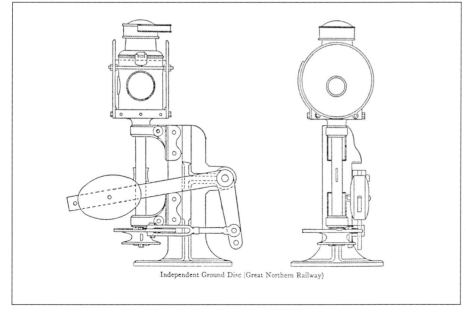

Independent Ground Disc (Great Northern Railway)

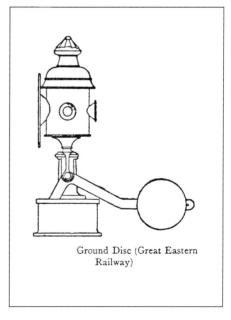

Ground Disc (Great Eastern Railway)

Above: The later style of ground signal, in the form of a disc, is seen here at Longbridge East on the old LMS/GWR Joint line. This example provides a driver with the authority to take any of four different routes; two or three discs were also common, but I have never seen five. *Graham Warburton*

Left: To emphasis the fact that older types of ground signal were long-lived, this example was photographed at Byfield, on the old SMJ section of the LMS, in November 1964. Many ground signals had miniature arms instead of discs, and sometimes more than one arm was attached to the same post where there was more than one route. Note that this former LNWR signal is off its home ground, not uncommon on the LMS where the structure of the signalling department did not follow the old pre-Grouping boundaries. The picture also suggests to modellers of rural branch lines that it is better to use old equipment rather than the latest item available; 'cascading' old but not life-expired equipment was commonplace throughout railway history. *Author's collection*

Right:
This rear view of a two-arm ground signal was photographed at Lower Darwin in October 1964, and is included to show the operating wires and the mechanism that interlocked the signals with the associated points. *Author's collection*

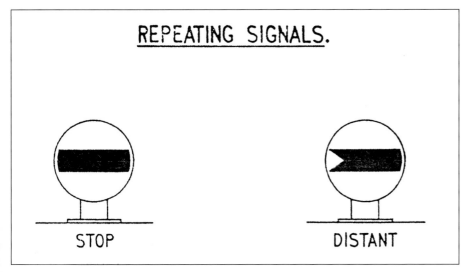

REPEATING SIGNALS.

STOP

DISTANT

Left: Repeating or banner signals were discs with a black bar, square-ended or 'fish-tailed' depending upon whether they were repeating a Stop or Distant signal, mounted on a post or bracket, depending upon their position.

Below left: This example of a banner signal on the platform at Dumfries was photographed in 1965. *Author's collection*

Banner repeating signals

Generally running signals were placed where it was possible for a driver to see them clearly, so that if they displayed the 'Stop' aspect he would be able to bring his train to a stand safely. However, at some locations the presence of bridges or other structures reduced the sighting distance, and where this happened a repeating signal was employed to tell the driver what aspect was displayed by the signal he was approaching. These signals took the form of a black banner on a white ground. They were also used at stations where, perhaps due to a curve in the platform, station buildings or bridges, the guard could not see the aspect of the Starting signal.

Diamond, 'D' and 'T' signs on signals

Before we consider colour light signals, the different signs found on some semaphore and colour light signals need to be explained. When a train came to a halt at a Stop signal, an appropriate sign, of which there were three types, advised the enginemen what further action was required:

White diamond: This denotes that a track circuit, depression bar or other device is protecting the train, so no action is required by the train crew to advise the signalman of their presence.

'D' sign: This indicates that a Fireman's Call Plunger is installed, which can be pressed by the fireman to advise the signalman that there is a train at the signal.

'T' sign: This indicates that there is a telephone adjacent to the signal, enabling the fireman to telephone the signalman to advise him that a train is at the signal.

If brought to a stand at a signal not displaying one of these signs, a member of the train crew was required to go to the signal box to inform the signalman of the presence of the train. Usually this was the fireman, and he signed the signal box register book and returned to the train after the signalman had placed a collar over the lever of the signal protecting the train. Where 'D' or 'T' signs were provided, the signalman would place a collar on the signal lever as a reminder, which prevented the signal being pulled off should he wrongly accept a further train – with track circuiting the signal would be locked electrically. The instructions governing this were complex and were known as Rule 55, Detention of Trains on Running Lines.

Stop shunt or Blasting signals

These were a throw-back to the early days of signalling, but were to be found well into BR days at Cadbury's in Birmingham and the Brush Works at Loughborough, with several also on the Burton on Trent brewery system and no doubt elsewhere. They were simply a horizontal board on top of a rotating post and were to be found at crossing points where two engines were shunting simultaneously. If the board was end-on, shunting could proceed, but if the board showed its full face, shunting had to stop on

that particular line. The signal could be operated from a cabin or simply a handle on the base of the post.

Another use for this type of signal was when a railway passed close to a quarry, as in the Peak District. The quarryman would notify the signalman that he wished to do some blasting and, if the line was clear, the signalman would give permission by turning the signal end-on; this action also locked the signal frame, meaning that no railway signals could be lowered until the blasting signal was reversed, again showing its full face to the quarryman.

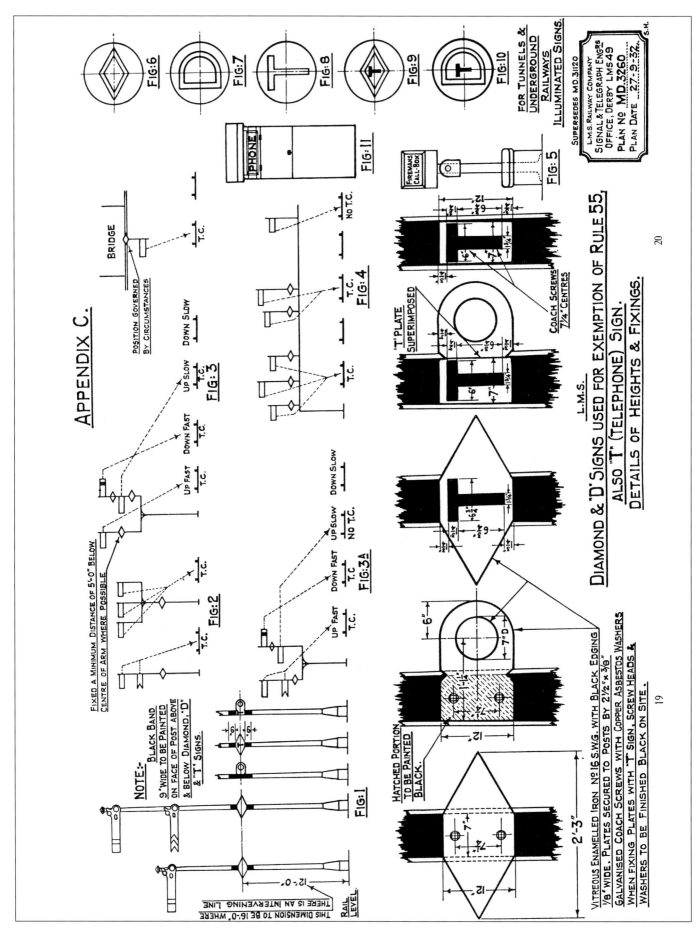

Left: On the subject of track circuit 'diamonds', this drawing, reproduced from the LMS's 'Instructions as to the Sighting of Signals' of April 1936, provides some useful information regarding the various white diamond, 'D' and 'T' signs used by the LMS in connection with Rule 55, with similar arrangements being applicable to the other major British railway companies.

Colour light signals

There are two types to consider, those with a separate lens for each aspect and the searchlight type, which has an electrically operated colour filter; as far as the driver is concerned both types display the same aspect. There was not, in my view, the rich variety of design that enabled colour light signals to be identified with a particular company, so, with the use of diagrams, I will concentrate on how they were used rather than try to show a number of similar designs.

The value of signals as an aid to increasing line capacity – that is to maximise the number of trains that can be run over a section of line in a given time – is almost as important as their role in terms of safety. Unfortunately, to achieve maximum line capacity all the trains need to run at the same speed and stop at the same stations. During the steam era this was not possible: at one extreme there were express passenger trains and at the other stopping freight trains that had to be shunted at most stations, and between these two extremes there was a variety of other trains to be accommodated. This led to the introduction of additional running lines, but where there were only two lines, one in each direction, the answer was to provide lie-bys or loops.

From an operational point of view, therefore, trains running at similar or identical speeds are to be preferred. On lines where there is an intense service of trains running at similar speeds, perhaps using electric traction, the three-aspect system is preferred. The accompanying diagrams show what happens when one, two or three Home signals are used.

Above right: This close-up view of a colour light signal was taken in 1972 and shows Carstairs No 1 Up Distant. *Graham Warburton*

Right: Station with one Home signal: the correct determination of the number and position of the Home signals at stations could reduce to a minimum the effect of the station stop. With only one Home signal, it will clear when the rear of the preceding train has passed beyond the Starting signal overlap, and this is the earliest time at which a second train may arrive at the sighting point of the Home signal if it is to have an uninterrupted run into the station.

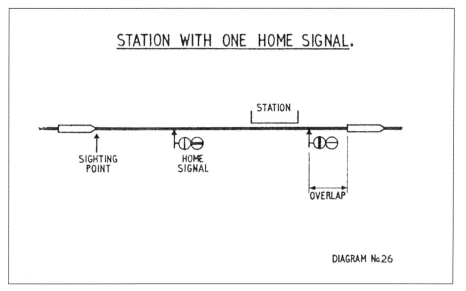

STATION WITH ONE HOME SIGNAL.

STATION

SIGHTING POINT   HOME SIGNAL   OVERLAP

DIAGRAM No.26

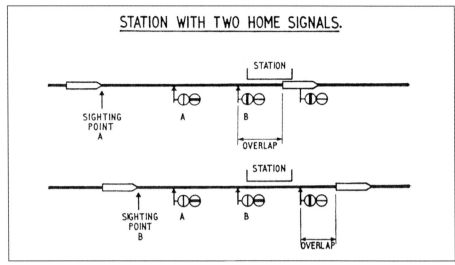

STATION WITH TWO HOME SIGNALS.

Left: Station with two Home signals: in this case the Outer Home signal clears when the rear of the train has passed beyond the overlap of the Inner Home signal, which allows a slightly reduced headway between trains. In a similar manner the Inner Home will clear after the rear of the preceding train has passed beyond the overlap of the Starting signal.

Centre left: Station with three Home signals: the introduction of an Intermediate Home signal allows an earlier clearance of signals than in the previous case.

Bottom: A modern layout of a junction with a main-line crossover and a siding connection using colour light signals and track circuiting. The numbers of the signals and their functions are also given.

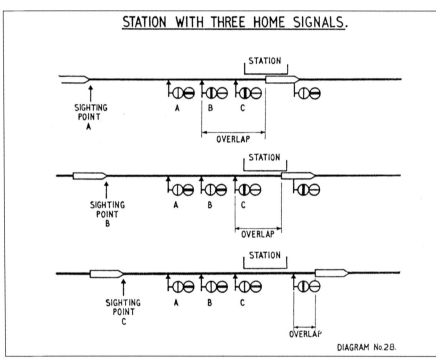

STATION WITH THREE HOME SIGNALS.

DIAGRAM No. 28.

The four-aspect system, first used on the Southern Railway, was provided for the benefit of steam trains running alongside electric trains. The much lighter and easier to stop electric train could easily stop on sighting a single yellow aspect, but the higher-speed steam-hauled express required a double yellow indication to give twice the braking distance to the Stop signal. Note also that three- or four-aspect colour light signalling coupled with full track circuiting does away with the Absolute Block, as every signal is a Distant signal, a situation that greatly increases track occupancy.

Multi-aspect signals

These can have three, four or five aspects. With a three-aspect signal, green is for 'Proceed', yellow for 'Caution' and red for 'Stop'. A four-aspect signal has green for 'Proceed', double yellow for 'Pass the next signal at restricted speed', single yellow for 'Caution' and red for 'Stop'. The five-aspect system incorporated a yellow-over-green indication meaning 'Pass second signal at restricted speed'. As far as I am aware, on the LMS only the Mirfield re-signalling in 1932 incorporated five aspects.

Multi-aspect signals are found on lines where there is a high traffic density and a mixture of types of train,

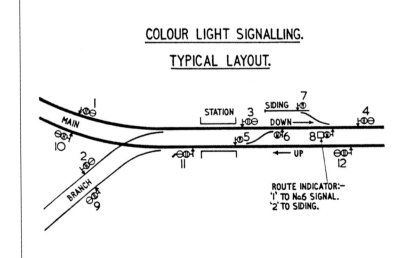

COLOUR LIGHT SIGNALLING.
TYPICAL LAYOUT.

ROUTE INDICATOR:—
'1' TO No.6 SIGNAL.
'2' TO SIDING.

1—Down main home
2—Down branch home
3—Down starting
4—Down advanced starting
5—Shunt up platform to down line
6—Shunt down line to up platform
7—Shunt siding to down line
8—Shunt down line to No. 6 signal or siding
9—Up branch advanced starting
10—Up main advanced starting
11—Up starting to branch or main
12—Up home

for example express passenger, stopping passenger and various classes of freight trains. Where there was sufficient space between a yellow and a red signal to provide the required braking distance for the fastest train that would run over the section of line, three-aspect signalling was installed, but if adequate braking distance could not be provided then four-aspect signalling was required. This usually applied if the position of junctions or stations did not allow the required 440-yard overlap. I have included some diagrams to illustrate how multi-aspect signals work.

Below: This drawing shows the sequence of aspects displayed by a three-aspect system. Note that the adequate braking distance between a yellow and red enables the fastest train to be safely brought to a stand.

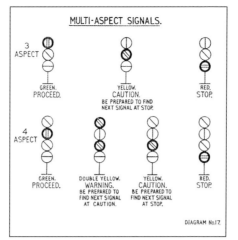

Left: The difference between the aspects of three-four-aspect colour light signals – the common aspect is that the red is the lower light on both types of signal.

Below: A typical arrangement of four-aspect signalling and the sequences displayed. The position of the signals is such that there is adequate braking distance between the signals displaying double yellow and red so that the fastest train may be brought to a stand without the danger of over-running the red signal, a circumstance commonly known today as a SPAD, or 'signal passed at danger'.

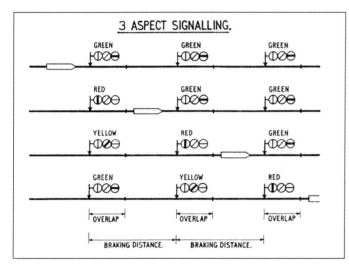

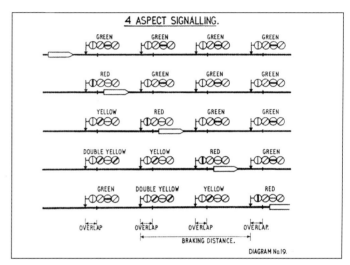

Latterly colour light signalling at junctions differed from semaphore signalling practice, but in earlier schemes colour lights were provided on 'dolls' as with semaphores. Then from the early 1930s 'position lights' were utilised, sometimes referred to as 'feathers'. In order to show how they were installed I have included diagrams with explanatory captions.

Right: This diagram appears in the LMS's 'Instructions as to the Sighting of Signals' of April 1936, showing early semaphore-pattern colour light signals. The instructions state that the colour light signal should be fixed as near as possible to the driver, ie always on the left-hand side of the track and at a minimum distance from his eye level in a vertical plane. Where space permits a post should conform to Fig 1, but it could be 14ft 6in above rail level if curvature of the track and a train on an adjoining line might interfere with the long-range view. Fig 2 was to be used where there was a junction in which the alternative routes are comparatively equal, the 'Y' indicator lights indicating the direction.

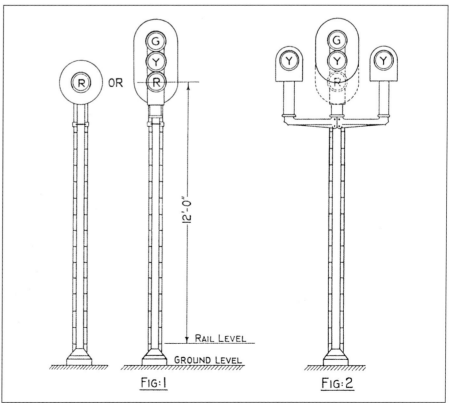

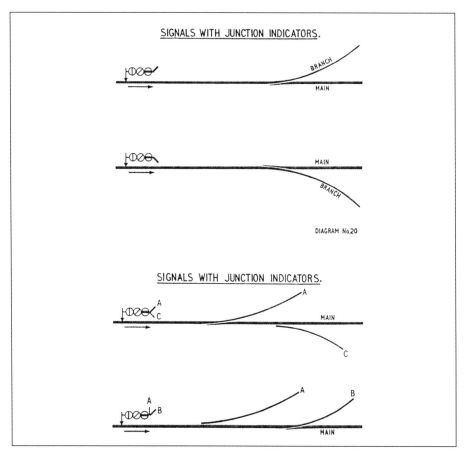

SIGNALS WITH JUNCTION INDICATORS.

BRANCH

MAIN

MAIN

BRANCH

DIAGRAM No.20

SIGNALS WITH JUNCTION INDICATORS.

A
C

A

MAIN

C

A

B

A

B

MAIN

Left: Modern practice is to arrange the signalling so that, in the normal course of events, a driver rarely encounters a red light. The arrangement of a single red light plus an indicator at a diverging junction is shown in these diagrams. The junction indicator takes the form of a row of white lights, generally three but possibly as many as five, arranged above the signal at an angle of 45 or 90 degrees from the vertical. The indicator projects to the left or right depending upon the direction of the diverging route. Where there is more than one diverging route the indicators are arranged as shown in the lower diagrams. It should be noted that when the road is set for the main, or, as it is often called, the high-speed route, the junction indicators are not displayed and the driver only sees a green light; this indicates that he is not required to reduce his speed, although if the junction is on a curve and there is a speed restriction on the main route, junction indicators would be provided.

Below: This picture, taken at Tweedmouth on 14 April 1963, records No 46474 on an SLS special, but is included to illustrate an illuminated route indicator above the colour light signal. *John Edgington*

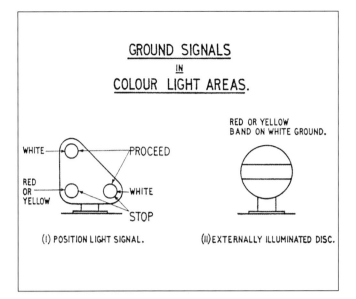

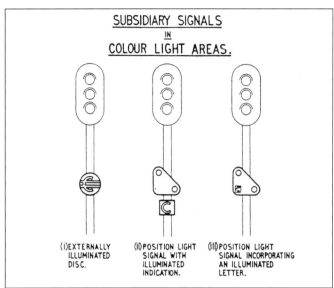

Colour light subsidiary, ground and repeating signals follow the same principles as semaphore signalling, although the method of illustrating the aspect is different.

Above: Two variations of ground signals in colour light areas: (i) position lights, a white light and a red or yellow light horizontally for 'Stop' and two white lights in the upper quadrant for 'Proceed'; and (ii) an externally illuminated disc with red or yellow bands on a white ground.

Above right: Subsidiary signals in colour light areas fulfilled a similar role to that of semaphore signals. They were arranged to be distinguishable from running signals, and this drawing shows three different variations: (i) an externally illuminated disc, with the letter 'S' (shunt ahead), 'C' (calling-on) or 'W' (warning) displayed on red parallel lines; (ii) position light signals with an internally illuminated sign displaying 'S', 'C' or 'W'; and (iii) a position light signal incorporating the appropriate illuminated 'S', 'C' or 'W'.

Below: Shunting wagons by gravity over a hump required co-operation between the shunters and signalmen and the driver of the shunting engine. In the most modern yards colour light signals would be used, but generally it was either hand signals or subsidiary semaphore signals. This picture shows shunting in progress at Toton, and illustrates a colour-light shunting signal. *National Railway Museum*

Telegraph poles

Closely allied to railway signalling was the railway telegraph and its associated poles that were to seen running alongside all steam railways. I am sure the older travellers will recall the way the wires went up and down past the carriage window as the train sped on its way! The wires not only carried speech, block bell and block instrument communication but also track circuit information, etc. Pyrometers were fitted to signal lamps that were out of the signalman's sight and gave information as to whether the flame in the lamp was in or out; the wires were connected to a repeater in the signal box and transmitted the information to the signalman. Power to light a signal lamp was also taken by the telegraph wires. Alongside most signal boxes there was a telegraph pole with wooden trunking bringing the cables into the box.

Modellers tend to neglect telegraph poles, and while I have yet to see a convincing method of representing the actual wires, the posts, cross arms and stays can certainly be reproduced accurately in model form. Poles came in three types – 'H', 'A' and single-pole form – the most common being the latter, while 'H' poles were seen on main lines where many pairs of wires were required. Poles were normally 50 to 60 yards apart; in 1935 the LMS stated that runs of 24 wires or more should be 60 yards apart, and up to 23 wires a maximum of 65 yards. Pole heights would range from 20 to 60 feet, with a minimum pole-top diameter of 5 to 9½ inches, and from 7¼ to 10¾ inches at ground level. All angle poles were stayed, and also most 'in line' poles. In 1935 the LMS required every pole with nine wires or more to be side-stayed, and every fifth pole to have four stays, ie stays in line and also at right angles to the line. For lines of eight wires or less, each pole was still side-stayed with a four-stayed pole every quarter of a mile. All terminal poles were stayed against line tension, and large 'H' poles may well have two or three stays on each leg. I cannot recall any model railway I have seen that had stays – most do not even have telegraph poles.

At underbridges (those that the railway passed beneath) the wires would either go over the top using tall poles, or through the bridge via brackets on the bridge sidewall; the latter arrangement would not be possible for a large number of wires, in which case the line would be terminated and cabled to another terminal pole at the far side of the bridge or tunnel.

Ground clearances were as follows: for occupation crossings, 16 feet; highway crossings, 20 feet; and railway tracks, 17 feet, increased to 20 feet by the LMS from 1938. Should a modeller manage to run realistic wires, the sag would be in the order of 12 inches for a 60-yard span at 60°F, more on a hot day, and less on a cold one! Pole steps commenced no lower than 10 feet above ground level and were placed alternately on opposite sides of the pole parallel to the arms and at 30-inch centres. The top step was 15 inches below the lowest arm, with two steps opposite each other 30 inches below the lowest arm.

Above: Note the rather splendid telegraph poles and the method of staying them and the signal on the old Midland Railway at Kegworth. The use of concrete for signal posts was not common, and this example is on the goods lines that ran behind the station. The passenger lines are to the left and the station signal box is alongside the up goods line. *Author's collection*

Above: The reason for including this picture is largely to show the telegraph posts and wires on each side of the tracks. This north-facing view could also have been used in Chapter 1, showing a section of the West Coast Main Line near Hemel Hempstead during the era before continuous welded track, and illustrates, left to right, the down fast, up fast, down slow and up slow lines. All are laid with 109lb flat-bottom rail on softwood sleepers with BRI fastenings (elastic spikes), except for the down slow, which appears to have Mills Clips fastenings. The only section of bullhead rail is a 95lb track panel on the down fast where the photographer is standing. Note that the tracks and cesses have been specially 'fettled up' for publicity photographs to be taken. *Martin Welch*

Below: Although telegraph poles do not figure prominently in this picture they are present. The most interesting part of this *c*1960 view is the arrangement of the bridges close to Sheffield Midland station. I have always felt that if they were on a model some viewers may think the arrangement was not realistic. Also of note are the ground signals required for local movements. *D. Ibbotson*

Chapter Three

Operating the Railway

In the two previous chapters I have outlined the development of permanent way and signalling, including some reference to the time interval system in order to provide readers with an understanding of the subject. In this chapter we will look at how track formations, signalling and train working come together, and how modellers can incorporate these features in their models. We will examine the various methods used from the time interval to the Absolute Block and explore single-line working. When planning this book it was tempting to use a number of separate chapters, but I eventually decided that it was too difficult to separate the related subjects, which is why this wide-ranging chapter has been subdivided. The emphasis has been placed upon what is relevant to modellers, which explains why some aspects, important on the full-size railway, have either been omitted or are only briefly mentioned.

A brief summary of some Requirements that could apply to modellers

Locking arrangements

Everything that was needed to run a railway was already in place by 1858. During the years that followed the materials and methods were refined and 'the Requirements', which had been established by that date, provided the basis that continues, with minor modifications, to the present day. One of the key elements is the interlocking of points to prevent conflicting routes being set.

The term 'interlocking' has been used previously, so perhaps an explanation is required. My favourite definition appears in the March 1910 *Railway Club Journal.*

Below: This picture taken at Cheltenham in about 1873 shows a hand-operated point (enlarged in inset) for part of a trailing crossover between the up and down main lines. Later this type of point would be worked from a signal box where the levers would be interlocked, but in the 1870s this did not apply to many parts of the British railway system. *Author's collection*

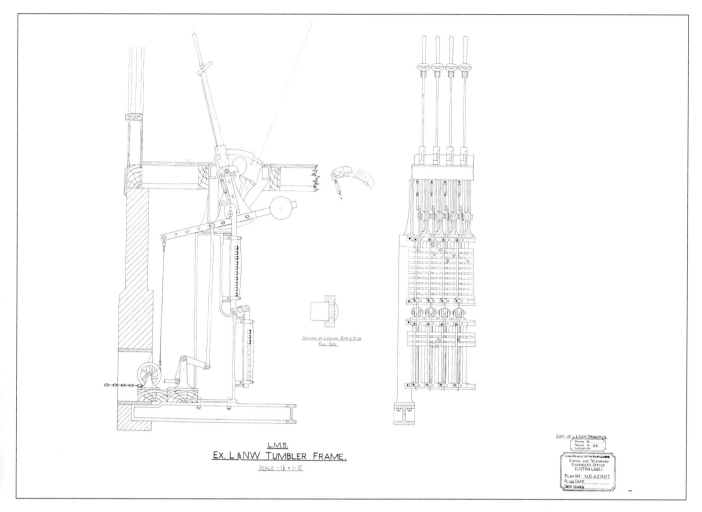

L.M.S.
Ex. L&NW TUMBLER FRAME.
SCALE · 1½" = 1'·0'

Above: An LNWR 'tumbler' frame with double locking racks. The drawing also shows the use of rocking levers, which were used to reverse the direction of movement of the racks. I have included this drawing in order to provide modellers who may wish to construct their own lever frame with an example of full-size practice. *LMS drawing in the author's collection*

Below: The track and signal layout at a 'simple wayside station', with a table explaining how the points and signals were mechanically interlocked. For example, before lever No 1 (the up Distant) can be pulled, lever No 2 (the Home), No 3 (the Starting signal) and No 4 (the Advanced Starting signal) must be pulled, so that the driver of an approaching train knows that when the Distant signal shows a 'Clear' aspect he has a clear run through station limits and through the block section as far as the Home signal for the next signal box in advance. Similarly, the disc signal that permits a train to reverse from the up line into the up siding (No 9) cannot be released to show a 'Clear' aspect until the points lever (No 8) has been pulled, which simultaneously locks levers Nos 3 and 7 in their normal positions. *Reproduced from* Modern Railway Working *Vol 6*

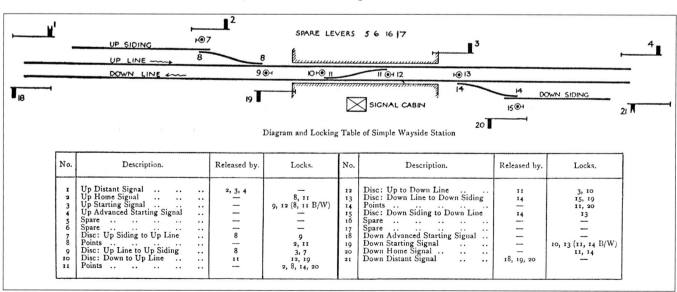

Diagram and Locking Table of Simple Wayside Station

No.	Description.	Released by.	Locks.	No.	Description.	Released by.	Locks.
1	Up Distant Signal	2, 3, 4	—	12	Disc: Up to Down Line	11	3, 10
2	Up Home Signal	—	8, 11	13	Disc: Down Line to Down Siding	14	15, 19
3	Up Starting Signal	—	9, 12 (8, 11 B/W)	14	Points	—	11, 20
4	Up Advanced Starting Signal ..	—	—	15	Disc: Down Siding to Down Line	14	13
5	Spare	—	—	16	Spare	—	—
6	Spare	—	—	17	Spare	—	—
7	Disc: Up Siding to Up Line ..	8	9	18	Down Advanced Starting Signal ..	—	—
8	Points	—	2, 11	19	Down Starting Signal	—	10, 13 (11, 14 B/W)
9	Disc: Up Line to Up Siding ..	8	3, 7	20	Down Home Signal	—	11, 14
10	Disc: Down to Up Line	11	12, 19	21	Down Distant Signal	18, 19, 20	—
11	Points	—	2, 8, 14, 20				

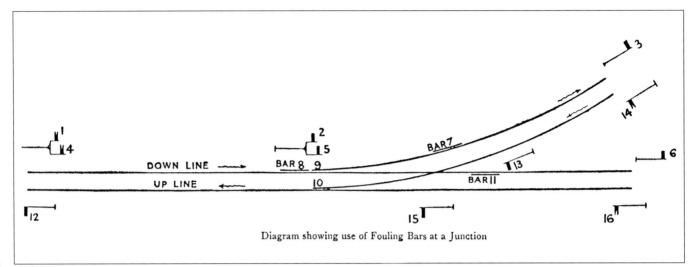

Diagram showing use of Fouling Bars at a Junction

Above: The fouling bars in this diagram (lever Nos 8, 7 and 11) were used to ascertain when the rear of a train was clear of the junction. For example, the facing points on the down line are worked by No 9 lever and locked by No 8 lever, which also works the locking bar. Likewise fouling bar lever No 11 has to be moved before Nos 2 and 13 signals can be pulled, and No 7 before signal 5 can be lowered. Note also that No 9 lever must be pulled before No 10, which works the up trailing junction points; this is to ensure that if a down train over-runs the junction signal it will be diverted on to the branch. *Reproduced from* Modern Railway Working *Vol 6.*

The principles and aim of interlocking may, however, be summed up by saying that if, at any given junction, a man entirely unacquainted with railway working were to enter the signal box, he might safely be allowed to manipulate the levers as he chose, in any manner, rational or irrational, without any collision between trains resulting, so long as the signals were obeyed.

But perhaps the best technical description is that given by Stanley Hall in his book *Railway Signalling in the British Isles: A Broad Survey*, who summarised the general principles as follows:

1 A lever working a main-line signal must be locked unless the levers working any points in the route to which the signal applies are in the proper position. (In other words, you cannot pull off the signal unless the points are set for the route to which the signal applies.)
2 When the signal lever movement has been made, all the levers concerned must be held in the required position. (The points cannot be changed to a different route if the signal is in the clear position for the route originally set.)
3 Signals permitting conflicting movements must lock each other.
4 Points must lock other points that might lead to a conflicting movement.

My method of describing interlocking states that when you operate my layout, the locking, both

Above: There are a number of interesting features to be seen in this 1910 picture of Oakamoor, a former North Staffordshire Railway station – and remember that the pace of change at stations on secondary lines was slow and many features to be see during the Edwardian era would be seen 50 years later, for example, the accommodation crossing connecting land in the same ownership on both sides of the line. Note the trailing crossover between the running lines and the connection between the main line and the goods sidings. *Author's collection*

Left: I find the simplicity of the layout of Penybont station on the Central Wales line most appealing – the double-track line with two passenger platforms, signal box and small goods yard is typical of many model railways. Note the modest facilities on the right-hand platform and the trailing crossover between the up and down line and goods yard, incorporating a single slip, with the barrow crossing laid through it. Further along the line, beyond the goods vans, there would be a trailing connection into the goods yard from the left-hand running line. Opposite the vans there is a trailing connection from either a loop line or lie-by. *Lens of Sutton*

mechanical and electrical, is so arranged that if the levers are not pulled or reversed in the correct sequence nothing will happen. The point to be made is that, in my opinion, more than anything else the interlocking of points and signals takes a model railway further along the path towards 'realism in miniature' – and on the prototype it is absolutely essential.

Interlocking developed over a number of years, and 'tappet' locking, introduced in 1874, was probably the most widely used method for interlocking signals with points. Also essential were locks on all facing points used by passenger trains, and methods to detect the presence of trains to prevent signals being pulled off if the points were not set. A locking bar was fitted to prevent facing points being moved under passing trains; this is a long bar fixed along the inside of the rail on the 'four-foot' side (ie between the rails). (For the record, the 'six-foot' is the term for the space between adjacent running lines.) The top of the locking bar is just below the flanges of passing wheels and it is operated by rodding from the signal box, being interlocked with the lever that operates the points; it can only be raised if no vehicle is occupying the track. Locking bars can be reproduced in model form, but other

than in larger scales it would almost certainly be in a non-working form. It is worth noting that early passenger stock was four- or six-wheeled, but with the introduction of bogie vehicles it became necessary to extend the length of locking bars.

Stations and gradients

The Requirements for stations were somewhat varied and depended upon when the station was built. For example, a station built at an early date that was not altered by the railway company would not have to comply with any requirements that were introduced later – the requirements were not retrospective. On the other hand, if the owning company made alterations that necessitated a Board of Trade inspection, the company might find that the Inspector required the company to comply with the current requirements. Stations built in later years might not have to comply with some old requirements that had been relaxed before it was constructed.

The following Requirements affect the design of station layouts and should be considered by modellers when designing a layout, although there were exceptions.

Left: The note on the rear of this undated picture states that it is looking south from Thornton viaduct (south end). Note the checkrails on both running lines. There is no indication of the gradient, but it requires catch points that remain open in order to derail any runaway vehicles. A 'Switch' sign or similar was always placed at these locations. *Author's collection*

Lines leading to passenger platforms should be arranged for use without reversal. Each line should have its own platform. At terminals a double line must not end as a single line (a rule added in 1928). The minimum width of platforms should be 6 feet at minor stations and 12 feet at major stations; a taper at the ends was allowed. Platform height should be 3 feet with a 12-inch overhang to provide a safety space, with additional space if required for point rod runs; platform ends should be ramped at 1 in 8. Light railway platforms do not need to be raised if the carriages have suitable steps.

When a station is built on, or near, a viaduct or bridge, a parapet or fence must be provided to prevent passengers who alight by mistake from falling. A clock must be provided, visible from the platforms (I have seen numerous Board of Trade inspection reports where the inspecting officer has drawn the railway company's attention to this requirement and sought confirmation that a clock would be installed). Although the Board of Trade would accept the construction of a station on a gradient steeper than 1 in 260, it did not like it and generally shunting was not permitted. If it was allowed, the engine had to be at the lower end of the train, and it was usual for the railway company to confirm that this would apply – the document, described as an 'undertaking' and under the railway company's seal, had to be lodged with the Board of Trade confirming that the requirement had been complied with.

Turntables are required at terminal stations unless trains are worked by suitable engines (tank engines) or by tender engines that are run at low speed on short journeys. There should be lighting at the turntable, and although it was not a requirement it was not unusual for water cranes or columns to be placed close to the turntables, and the provision of an inspection pit was not uncommon. If the turntable is not at a safe distance from adjacent lines, the turntable bolt is to be interlocked in the signal lever frame.

Left: Although this does not really count as a bridge there is a lesson to be learned from this picture of ex-LNWR '19-inch Goods' No 8734 at the head of an excursion train. The photograph was taken in 1936 at Conway Castle, where the line passes through the castle walls. Note the arrangement of the signal post, with the lower arm about halfway up in order to provide sighting through the arch. The position of signals and the ability of the driver to be able to see the arm is very important on the full-size railway, and it should also apply on the model. *Author's collection*

Bridges

There are three features regarding of bridges that concern modellers. First, parapets must be at least 4ft 6in high, including any steel girders that form part of them. Second, important bridges and viaducts must have wheel guards or raised checkrails to constrain derailed wheels. (But how was 'important' defined? In Scotland, the interpretation differed between ex-LMS and ex-LNER lines as late as the 1990s, and may still apply.) Third, refuges must be provided on long viaducts and in tunnels. Readers may find *Bridges for Modellers* (see the References) very helpful when planning this aspect of their layouts.

Above: When describing bridges in relation to the railway, one that the line passes beneath is an underbridge and one that the railway crosses is an overbridge. This underbridge is at Heysham on the old Midland branch from Lancaster. I have always felt that bridges made from stone are particularly attractive when suitably weathered, as seen in this 1974 picture. *D. Ibbotson*

Right: As a variation to a bridge carrying a road over a railway or a railway over a road, this picture of University Road bridge in Birmingham shows a bridge that carried a road over both a railway and canal; an interesting feature for a model. *Author's collection*

Track layouts and permanent way

The first chapter covered many aspects of permanent way, but there are some important aspects of the Requirements that need to be mentioned.

First, junctions of single lines should be formed as double-line junctions; although this requirement had gone by 1925, many original layouts remained in place until the lines were closed. On page 75 is a picture of one of my favourite railway locations, Broom Junction, as an example of this arrangement.

Second, sidings should be arranged to minimise the use of running lines for shunting. Although this stipulation was very desirable, often it did not happen, and awkward layouts remained until a station was closed for goods traffic or the line was closed entirely.

Third, the number of facing points was to be kept to the minimum, and they should be as close as possible to the signal box. Following the development

of point motors, this ceased to be a requirement in 1925.

Over the years considerable emphasis was placed on reminder apparatus, which included detector bars for standing vehicles, for example at a station platform. Considerable use was made of electricity for detection and reminder purposes from an early date, but generally this would not apply to most model railways, although the inclusion of detector bars on a large layout would add to the realism for the operators.

Two features not discussed in Chapter 1 regarding the permanent way are illustrated here. Checkrails should be provided on curves on passenger lines whose radii are less than 10 chains (220 yards), or 8 chains (176 yards) for light railways. Most curves on model railways are too sharp, so judgement must be made, but the use of checkrails can be helpful, and illustrations showing this feature have been included. Second, fixed diamond crossings must not be flatter than 1 in 8, otherwise switch diamonds must be used and worked as additional facing points.

Above: This picture was taken at Bridlington in 1958, and has been included to draw attention to the 'flow' of trackwork and the signal gantry with signals for trains travelling in both directions.
John Edgington

Below left: Apart from providing a rear view of the 15 and 20mph speed restriction signs on the left-hand signal gantry, this picture shows a nice industrial railway scene. Photographed in September 1963 at Tyne Dock, it confirms that 40 years after the 1923 Grouping former North Eastern Railway signals were still in use. *John Edgington*

Above right: There are some useful features to be found in this picture, taken near the junction of the Welbeck Colliery branch and the line between Mansfield and Langwith on the old Midland Railway in 1929. To the right is an example of a new upper-quadrant signal mounted on a wooden post with the white diamond sign to indicate that the line is track circuited, and some cable trunking. Note on the left the fogman's hut and brick-built stove, together with the device for placing a detonator on the line when required during foggy conditions. The bridge in the distance carried the LNER line from Chesterfield to Lincoln over what was now the LMS.
NRM, Derby Collection, DY 15401

Right: I have included this drawing of a typical fogman's hut to provide modellers with the dimensions of this common item to be found on all British railways during the steam era.

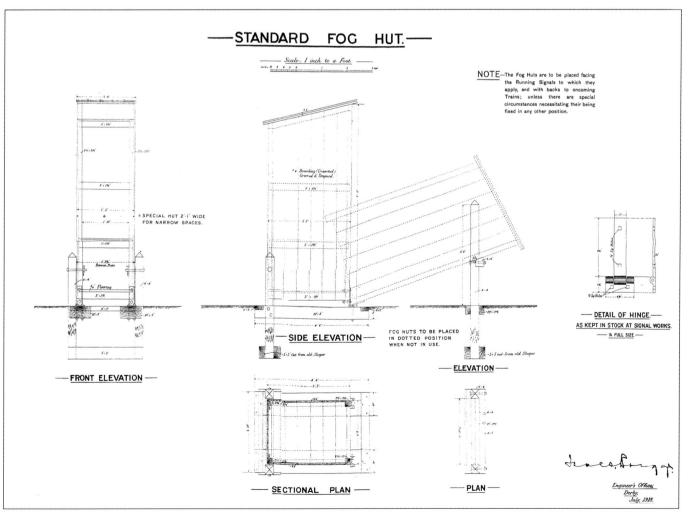

—STANDARD FOG HUT.—

Scale. 1 inch to a Foot.

NOTE—The Fog Huts are to be placed facing the Running Signals to which they apply, and with backs to oncoming Trains; unless there are special circumstances necessitating their being fixed in any other position.

* SPECIAL HUT 2'-1" WIDE FOR NARROW SPACES.

— FRONT ELEVATION —

— SIDE ELEVATION —

FOG HUTS TO BE PLACED IN DOTTED POSITION WHEN NOT IN USE.

— ELEVATION —

— DETAIL OF HINGE —
AS KEPT IN STOCK AT SIGNAL WORKS.
¼ FULL SIZE

— SECTIONAL PLAN —

— PLAN —

Engineer's Offices
Derby,
July, 1918.

Left: Although there is also a fogman's hut to be seen here, the reason for including this picture is to draw attention to the arrangements at the end of the platform. Note that the Starting signal is on a bracket in order to ensure a clear view for the driver of an approaching train, with a Distant signal below and the white diamond to indicate that the line is track circuited. Where there were water columns, cranes or, as seen here, a 'parachute' tank to allow enginemen to take water, other features would also be seen: a lamp was essential, and a brazier, kept alight in cold weather to prevent the water from freezing, was commonplace. I do not know the location of this picture, but believe it is somewhere on the old Lancashire & Yorkshire Railway.
British Railways

Below: This picture returns me to one of my favourite themes, the arrangement of ballast on model railways. All too often it is not realistic. This picture, taken at Tunbridge Wells in 1907, illustrates how in engine sheds the ballast came over the top of sleepers, although in later years it would be more likely to be only to the top of the sleepers, not over them. However, what did not change was that the ground between the tracks was generally ash, as seen here, and not ballast. *NRM, F. Burtt collection*

Right: The Requirements stated that a junction between single lines should be formed as double junctions, which can only be done when one single line is doubled for a short distance. Broom Junction in Warwickshire has always been one of my favourite locations, and illustrates this principle. To the left is the branch to Stratford-upon-Avon, while the line to Evesham is straight on behind the line of wagons, which are standing on a siding; note the trap points to protect the running line from any wagons that may run along the siding and foul the main line. The sidings were used for exchange traffic between the Stratford and Evesham lines. *Author's collection*

Below: Junctions were where lines converged or diverged, depending upon the direction of travel, but the term also applied to locations where different classes of running line came together. This 1950 north-facing view of New Mills South Junction shows how this type of junction was arranged, together with the associated signalling. *L&GRP*

Left: Skelton Junction is near Altrincham on the CLC. Straight ahead is the CLC line to Liverpool, while the line to the left leads to a junction with the LNWR and that to the right was a burrowing junction that passed beneath the Liverpool line and went to Altrincham. There are also a few sidings to be seen, probably used for exchange purposes. Apart from drawing attention to the way the junctions are laid, the main reason for including this picture was to show a tall signal box, built to enable the signalman to have a good view of all the lines he controlled. *L&GRP*

Centre left: Although I doubt if many modellers would have the space to build a junction like that seen in this 1948 view of Ashby Junction, it does show a form of layout where there was a junction between a double-track and a four-track line. *John Edgington*

Below left: Again, there cannot be many modellers who would be able to build the number of sidings shown in this 1910 view of Chilwell sidings, Toton, but the principles behind the layout can be followed. The points to note are that the shunting neck, or head shunt, leads directly to the 'king point', which, depending upon how it is set, will direct wagons to the groups of sidings to the left and right. As can be seen, the sidings are in groups and, subject to space, were laid out to facilitate ease of working. *Author's collection*

Above right: I have used the term 'flow' to describe the curves in trackwork on the full-size railway, and this diagram shows how the concept also applies to sidings. The source of the drawings specifies the following: gain as much standing room for wagons as the shape of the land will allow; and ensure easy and regular running on all routes using curves of a constant radius.

Figs 1-3 show various systems of arranging the 'gathering line' and connections, while a single-tongue trap point is shown at Fig 5 and a 'straddle' switch at Fig 4. I am not sure how widespread the use of the latter device was, but when it was open the track gauge widened and a runaway would become derailed. Other aspects to note are, in Fig 1, the trap points into the short siding or shunting neck, and in Fig 2 the alternative way that the connections from the main line can be arranged. *Reproduced from* Railway Permanent Way

Right: Checkrails on sharp bends on running lines were not common, but since modellers have to use tight curves in order to build a layout to fit the space available, they could be made a feature. These checkrails are seen on the Lifford curve at Lifford West Junction, Birmingham, in 1959. An up express behind No 45656 is heading for Birmingham, while No 42816 waits with a train of empty vans for Cadbury's. Note the trap points to the left of the 2-6-0. Finally it is worth pointing out that this curve was also used by passenger trains. *Roger Shelton*

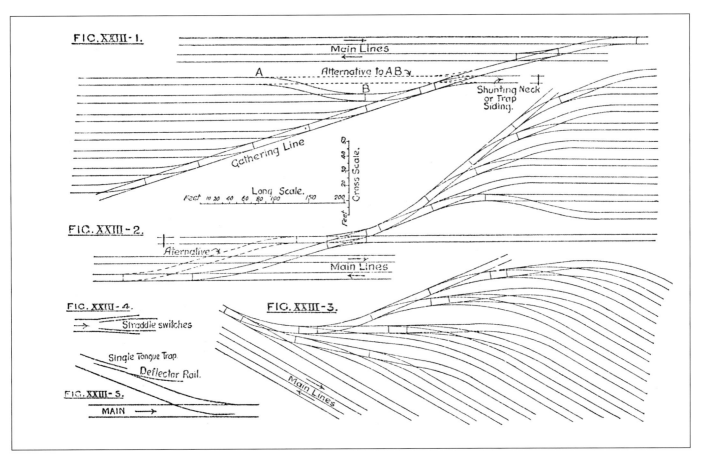

FIG. XXIII-1.

Main Lines

A — Alternative to A.B. —

B

Shunting Neck or Trap Siding.

Gathering Line

Cross Scale.

Long Scale.

Feet 10 20 40 60 80 100 150 200

FIG. XXIII-2.

Alternative

Main Lines

FIG. XXIII-4.

Straddle switches

Single Tongue Trap.

Deflector Rail.

FIG. XXIII-5.

MAIN

FIG. XXIII-3.

Main Lines

Safety points

Safety points – such as trap or catch points – have already been mentioned on a number of occasions, in particular at junctions between goods and passenger lines, but they were also required on lines having gradients steeper than 1 in 260, in order to catch vehicles or trains that break or run away. In view of the fact that most modellers avoid gradients on their layouts, they are unlikely to be used, but we should be aware of them.

The Requirements imposed a discipline on the design and operation of safety points, particularly at busy stations where many movements were required. For example, up and down fast, slow, independent and carriage lines might be required, with parallel double junctions for flexibility of movement. This method of working was a complete contrast to continental practice during the same period, where bi-directional running was normal, as it is today on the present-day railway system in the United Kingdom

Above: There are a number of things to be seen on this 1952 picture of Thurso, a former Highland Railway station. Note the facing point lock and cover on the left-hand line and at the points beyond, but the main reason for including the picture was to show the safety points. Note how trap points protect the passenger lines where there is a connection with a goods line. The trap point is open on the line from the goods shed, on the right of the picture, but that on the line from the goods yard is closed to enable the 'Ben' Class 4-4-0 to run forward.
R. S. Carpenter collection

Below: This example of trap points was taken at Lenton Junction South in 1913, and shows them being worked in conjunction with a facing point lock to protect the main line. *Author's collection*

Left: A variation of a trap point that just derailed a vehicle was a 'blind siding', a term used to describe a short siding that acted as a trap but was not really long enough to hold a vehicle without fouling the adjoining lines. These were commonplace at the end of a loop line where the loop rejoined the running line. *Author's collection*

Below: Dornoch was a small terminus station, and the arrangement seen in this September 1953 view is rather interesting. The trap point on the run-round line in the left centre is worked by the point rod on the right; note how the rod goes over the base of the hand point that sets the road for either the goods shed or the siding to the right of the picture. *Brian Hilton*

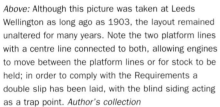

Above: Although this picture was taken at Leeds Wellington as long ago as 1903, the layout remained unaltered for many years. Note the two platform lines with a centre line connected to both, allowing engines to move between the platform lines or for stock to be held; in order to comply with the Requirements a double slip has been laid, with the blind siding acting as a trap point. *Author's collection*

Below: Another form of protection to prevent rolling-stock from unauthorised movements was the scotch block, described in Chapter 1. This picture, taken at Victoria Dock, London, in 1922 shows scotch blocks positioned to prevent wagons running on to the public highway, operated by the lever seen on the left. *Author's collection*

Above: Signs were used to show the location of catch points; this rather splendid example was photographed at Kineton on the old SMJ line in 1964. *Author's collection*

	Usual.	.... Ry.
CHAPTER II.		
Passenger Platforms. (Fig. II.–1)– Height (H on Fig. II.–1) of Platform above rail, measured at right angles to a line across the tops of the two rails of the track	3′ 0″	
Clearance (C Fig. II.–1) from outer edge of rail, to nose of platform coping, on straight road........	2′ 1″	
Ditto on curves, add to ′– ″† the versed sine on a chord of... (This clearance to be measured to a line at right angles to the surface of the track rails.)	40′ 0″	
Overhang of coping from wall face	1′ 0″*	
Cross fall, away from track, of coping	1 in 72	
Ditto of platform behind coping	1 in 36	
Nearest distance of pillars, etc., from edge of platform............	6′ 0″*	
Width of platform, small stations	6′ 0″*	
Do. Do. large Do.	12′ 0″*	
Inclination of ramped ends........	1 in 8 *	

* B. of T. Requirements. † Usual about 1 ft. 11 ins.

When a line at a platform changes directly from the straight to a sharp curve, the extra clearance necessary to the curved portion, should be obtained by moving the wall line gradually away from the rail on the straight. Care will be necessary to get an "eyeable" line on the coping and still retain the correct alignment of the rails. A transition curve on the rails avoids this difficulty.

14

	Usual.	.... Ry.
		MISCELLANEOUS.
Goods and Mineral Loading Stages. Height above Rail of :—		
Stage for loading and unloading general goods ...	3′ 6″	
Cattle Stage	3′ 6″	
Horse Stage	3′ 6″	
Stage for loading high side wagons with minerals etc. from carts by tipping......	8′ 0″ to 9′ 6″	
Stage for coaling Loco's......	5′ 0″	
The side clearances from rail are usually made 1 inch more than as required for passenger platforms.		
Carriage Loading Docks. *For transferring road vehicles to and from railway stock over the end of the latter.* Height above rail	4′ 0″	
Cart Weighing Machines.		*
Length of table	14′ 0″	20′ 0″
Width of table	8′ 0″	8′ 0″
Tonnage	15tons	20 tons
Wagon Weighing Machines.		
Length of table	14′ 0″	
Tonnage	20 tons	
Distance apart of Weighing and "Dead" Rails	1′ 0″	
Water Column or Water Crane.		
Space required when column is between tracks	11′ 0″	
Distance from rail to centre of column, when column is to outside of tracks ...	6′ 6″	
Distance of Water Column behind signal of line on which engine takes water	60′ 0″	

* For Road Motor Vehicles.

15

Clearances

There are clearly specified measurements for clearances and these that applied in 1922 are shown in the accompanying table. One problem that modellers have to contend with is that when moving away from an exact scale standard and using a modelling standard, adjustments have to be made. For example, in the popular 4mm scale OO gauge model locomotives and rolling-stock are built to a scale of 4mm to 1 foot, but the track is built to a scale of 3.5mm to 1 foot. This causes problems with clearances between parallel tracks, in particular on curves, and as a result some form of compromise is required, such as an increased distance between tracks. Therefore I consider that it makes more sense to give prototype dimensions and leave it to modellers to make their own adjustments.

Road and accommodation crossings

Public level crossing gates close across the railway, but occupation and accommodation crossing gates open away from the line. An occupation crossing is provided where a railway intersects an occupier's existing private road, while an accommodation crossing is provided to link occupiers' property that is bisected by a railway, the right being lost if the ownership is later split. These definitions apply to bridges as well as level crossings. Should sidings be connected to running lines near level crossings, the points should be not less than 100 yards from the crossing.

Above & overleaf: One problem that modellers encounter is lack of space. While this book was in preparation I was assisting a group of modellers in constructing a new layout, and reference to these tables in *Railway Permanent Way* was frequent, and they were very useful. The dimensions given are, of course, for the full-size railway and need to be adjusted for the various scales, in particular with N and OO where the scale used for the track is not the same as that used for everything else. *Reproduced from Railway Permanent Way*

CHAPTER II.

	Usual.	.... Ry.
Water Troughs.		
Height of rim above rail ..	3″	
Height of water above rail...	2″	
Gradient of track towards ends of troughs	1 in 300	
Gradient of trough at ends	1 in 192	
Engine Turntables. †		
Present standard diameter	65′ 0″	
Other diameters of tables in use		
Space between rim of table and an adjacent track ...	9′ 0″	
Wagon Turntables. †		
Present standard diameter	13′ 0″	
Other diameters in use......		
Engine Pits.		
Width between side walls...	3′ 9″	
Depth of Pit floor below rail level. "Inside" pit......	2′ 2″ to 2′ 5″	
Depth of Pit floor below rail level. "Outside" pit ...	3′ 0″ to 3′ 3″	
Carriage Pits.		
Width between side walls...	3′ 9″	
Depth of pit floor below rail level. Steam Stock	2′ 6″ to 3′ 0″	
Depth of pit floor below rail level. Electric Stock ...	3′ 4″	
Overbridges.		
Minimum clear span or opening for single line ...	13′ 8″ ‡	
Desirable clear span or opening for single line ...	15′ 6″ ¶	

† All tracks approaching a turntable should be laid straight for a length adjacent to the table, equal to the diameter of the table. This straight must be in line with the table rails when turned towards it.

‡ 4′ 3″ clearance ; should not be used on new work.

¶ 5′ 2″ clearance.

16

MISCELLANEOUS.

	Usual.	.... Ry.
Overbridges—*con.*		
Minimum clear span or opening for double line ...	24′ 10″ ‡	
Desirable clear span or opening for double line ...	26′ 6″ §	
Minimum clear span or opening for four lines with one 10′ 0″ space ...	51′ 2″ ‡	
Desirable clear span or opening for four lines with one 10′ 6″ space ...	53′ 6″ ¶	
Minimum headway	14′ 6″	
Desirable headway	15′ 0″	
Width between parapets, Turnpike road	35′ 0″ ‖	
Width between parapets, Public carriage road	25′ 0″ ‖	
Width between parapets, Private road	12′ 0″ ‖	
Height of parapets	4′ 0″ ‖	
Underbridges.		
Headway.—Turnpike road, for centre 12 ft. of arch	16′ 0″ ‖	
Public carriage road, for centre 10 ft. of arch	15′ 0″ ‖	
Private road, for centre 9 ft. of arch	14′ 0″ ‖	
Widths of roadway	As for overbridges ‖	
Height of parapets	4′ 6″ ‖	
Desirable width between parapets, for single line...	15′ 6″ ¶	
Desirable width between parapets, for double line...	26′ 6″ §	

‡ 4′ 3″ clearance ; should not be used on new work.

§ 5′ 1″ clearance.

‖ Minimum under Railway Clauses Consolidation Act, 1845, and subject to objection by Road Authorities.

The bridge openings given are for straight tracks.

¶ 5′ 2″ clearance.

17

Left: When reference is made to a 'crossing', it is usually a level crossing, where a public road crosses the railway on the same level. The control of trains and road traffic is in the hands of a signalman, or in some cases a person who acts under the instructions of the signalman. There are also 'accommodation' crossings, provided when the land on both sides of the railway is in the same ownership and the owner is allowed to cross. This picture was taken at Ilkeston Junction in 1911, but similar crossings existed all over Great Britain until the end of steam and later. It shows a timber boarded crossing over five running lines. Note that when the gate is open it swings away from the line and a 'Beware of the Trains' notice is required. *Author's collection*

Level crossings

Until the coming of the automatic half-barrier, the protection for level crossings remained as established in 1858, with red discs or targets on the gates for daylight and red lamps at night, rotating with the gates unless the view of the enginemen is inadequate, in which case Distant signals were also to be provided; if the Distant signals were worked, they must be interlocked with the gates. While the Requirements stated that Stop signals were only required at important level crossings, the practices of the various railway companies varied. These were not, however, section signals, unless the gate box was also a block post. If it was, and the level crossing was in the overlap, the gates would have to be opened for a train to approach even if it did not subsequently pass the protecting signal. There are examples of this arrangement at a number of stations where the protecting signal was also the section Home. Once the passenger train had stopped, the gates could be opened again for the roadway until the train was ready to depart, or, in the case of a goods train, it might have set back into a refuge siding.

If there was a Stop signal at a level crossing but it was not a section Home, no overlap would be required and motorists would just hope that the engine driver would always be able to stop! Signals might be required at level crossings on 'one engine in steam' lines, even though there were no signals on the line for any other purpose. At many major level crossings a pedestrian footbridge was provided.

Top right: The rather unusual arrangement seen in this c1960 view of the east end of Llanelly station is worthy of note for a modeller who wants something a little different – the turnout incorporates a reverse curve to avoid points in the level crossing. There is a long checkrail to the left, and a very short blind siding. *Martin Welch*

Centre right: The level crossing at Woburn Sands on the LNWR line from Oxford to Cambridge was photographed in 1967 and represents a level crossing on a secondary cross-country branch line. *Author's collection*

Right: Worksop is an ex-Great Central station and I have included this August 1964 picture to illustrate features typical of a level crossing over a double-track line at a station. The road crossing is just beyond the end of the platform and the signal box, Worksop East, is close to the crossing. The signal box steps are facing approaching traffic, and although this was the common arrangement there are many examples of signal boxes where the steps are at the other end. There is also a pedestrian footbridge, which would usually feature a warning notice to passengers not to cross the line on the level, and there is a barrow crossing alongside the road. There is also a 'parachute' water tank, which was not as commonplace as a water crane or water column. *H. B. Priestley*

Left: Countesthorpe was on the former Midland line from Wigston to Rugby, and this picture was taken in about 1958. The level crossing incorporates a barrow crossing, which is part of the timber-built roadway laid between the platforms. The signal box is on the platform, and its steps cannot be seen. Note the substantial post from which the gates hang. There are a number of diagrams of crossing gates in various books, but the only railway company drawing of a crossing known to me appears in *Midland Record* 15 (see Appendix 2).
D. Ibbotson

Below: Long Eaton is on the former Midland Railway Erewash line near Toton. This picture shows the mechanism used to operate the gates, which unusually is uncovered here. The roadway appears to have a metal surface, and again this was not uncommon; the material used would depend upon the date and importance of the road. *Author's collection*

Right: In many respects this 1949 picture of Laxfield station, the terminus of the Mid Suffolk Light Railway, is typical of crossings that appear on model railways where there is no signal box and no signals – being a light railway the requirements were less rigid. *Author's collection*

Below: This drawing of typical level crossing gates provides an example of wooden construction. The length of the gates varies according to the width of the road, and they might be square to the road or at an angle. On a square crossing the length of a gate would be 14 feet from the centre of the shaft to the end of the gate, less three-quarters of an inch each to allow a 1½-inch clearance between the gate toes. This allowance also prevents binding should any slight movement or dropping of the gates occur. *Reproduced from* Railway Signalling and Communications

Below right: A gate catch lock and its method of working. *Reproduced from* Railway Signalling and Communications

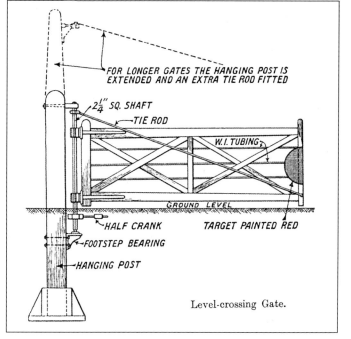

FOR LONGER GATES THE HANGING POST IS EXTENDED AND AN EXTRA TIE ROD FITTED

2¼" SQ. SHAFT

TIE ROD

W.I. TUBING

GROUND LEVEL

HALF CRANK

TARGET PAINTED RED

FOOTSTEP BEARING

HANGING POST

Level-crossing Gate.

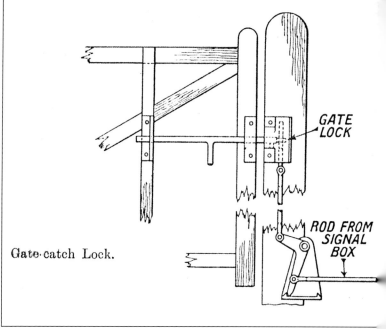

GATE LOCK

ROD FROM SIGNAL BOX

Gate-catch Lock.

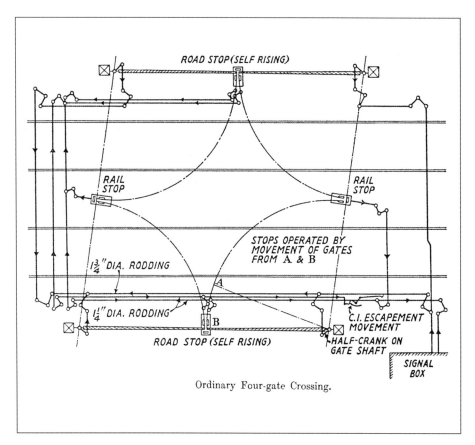

ROAD STOP (SELF RISING)

RAIL STOP

RAIL STOP

STOPS OPERATED BY
MOVEMENT OF GATES
FROM A & B

1¾" DIA. RODDING

1¼" DIA. RODDING

A

B

C.I. ESCAPEMENT
MOVEMENT

HALF-CRANK ON
GATE SHAFT

SIGNAL
BOX

ROAD STOP (SELF RISING)

Ordinary Four-gate Crossing.

Other lineside features

Fencing is a definite requirement when modelling any British railway – I believe this is the only country where it is a legal requirement. Modelling a wire fence is rather difficult, while the railway companies had their own styles of wooden fencing. Other than suggesting that modellers interested in total accuracy should investigate this subject further,

it is not, as far as I am aware, a subject that has attracted much attention in the model press, but details of Midland Railway fencing will be found in *Midland Record* 18.

Finally, every railway must still be equipped with mile, half-mile, quarter-mile and gradient posts. Trespass notices and other signs should also not be overlooked, but we are perhaps moving away from the main subject.

Left: This drawing shows an ordinary crossing with four gates, the necessary connections for working them, and the stops that hold the gates in position. When a single rod is used for working gates, either 1¾-inch tubular or ordinary channel iron is employed. The standard sizes for gate rodding are 1¾ inches external diameter for tubing, and 1½ inches diameter for solid rod when necessary, as in the case of the 1½-inch joints for the gate cranks and the screwed ends for the adjusting couplings. Ordinary channel point rodding might be used, but tubular rodding is the preferred method. In the drawing the cross-rods from the gates are of 1¾-inch tubing, being single rods. The gate cranks are of a strong and heavy design.

Gate stops are necessary to stop the gates and hold them in position, either normal or reverse, for although the rodding is strong enough to operate the gates, it will not prevent them from over-running or being forced out of position by springing the connections. Stops are of two kinds, one pattern being fixed in the roadway to hold the gates across the road, the other, fixed in the 'six-foot', to hold the gates across the railway. Both types are similar in design, but the road stops are so arranged and operated that when the gates are swung to close the roadway the stops do not rise and form an obstruction thereon until the gates are close to them; this is called delayed action. Each stopbox is provided with front stops, one for each gate, and a back stop that is made wide enough to take both gates. When the road stops are raised the rail stops are down and vice versa; when in the raised position both are locked by the final movement of the stop lever in the signal box and are incapable of being depressed. The front stops are counter-balanced and, until finally locked, can be forced down by the toes of the gates passing over them, rising again as soon as the gates are inside and preventing them from swinging back after striking the back stop. The rail stops are operated by one rod, which raises or lowers the stops and locks or unlocks them, according to the position of the stop lever. The road stops each require two operating rods, one from the stop lever for locking and unlocking and for lowering the front stops when the gates require to be placed across the railway, the other to raise the front and back stops when the gates are swung to close the roadway and to lower the back stops when the gates are returning to close the railway. *Reproduced from Railway Signalling and Communications*

Left: The gate wheel inside Dunhampstead signal box, on the Birmingham to Gloucester line of the Midland Railway. Some level crossing gates were opened and closed manually, but a wheel inside the signal box controlled others. *R. S. Carpenter*

Working the line

Time interval and Absolute Block

In Chapter 2 I explained that early signalling was based on trains being signalled from station to station, at first by time interval, then later by space interval, with messages exchanged by simple telegraph. The person in charge went round setting the points, then when the time had passed or the message came that the next station would accept the train, he pulled off the signal and the train departed. Whether the next station was ready for the train remained to be seen – the driver had to look out for the signal and, if it was red, stop short of the station, which might still be unprepared for it, with points not set or even a train standing on the line in front. Distant signals, giving early warning of the state of the section ahead, began to be used in the mid-1840s.

The publication of the first edition of the Board of Trade Requirements in 1858 stated that all new lines built thereafter had to have Stop and Distant signals in both directions, and their levers, together with the levers of the relevant switches (points), must be brought together and worked together, ie interlocked. The Board of Trade tried to encourage the adoption of these measures and, in particular, Absolute Block working on existing lines, and even tried to get an Act to enforce this in 1873. However, the Act that was passed only sought annual returns from the companies showing the progress made.

Companies had been making progress on busy lines because Absolute Block working meant that more trains could be run, and thus more revenue generated. Public reaction to the Armagh accident allowed the Board of Trade to push through the Regulation of Railways Act 1889, making block working, interlocking and continuous automatic brakes on passenger trains compulsory. By 1895 more than 99% of the signalling at stations was interlocked, and block working was almost universal on the British railway system. The Act and the 1892 Requirements arising from it state the principle that an adequate interval of space must be ensured, by block telegraph, between following trains and, in the case of a junction, between converging or crossing trains. Telephone communication was accepted later for light railways.

The Requirements went into further detail on matters such as number, position and colour of Distant signals, the colour of front lights – red, yellow and green – and thus by implication the colour of Stop arms. They did not stipulate how many Stop arms were needed at each station, and it was left to the companies to devise the signalling regulations needed to ensure that the principle was met. The companies were also urged to standardise the principles of signalling and block working, and by 1887 a committee had been established, whose deliberations were finalised by the Railway Clearing House as a set of 30 standards on 3 March 1893. The key distinction from early signalling was that the Absolute Block section was between the two stations, or block posts, concerned; movements in the station areas could be controlled by various signals or hand signals; and a departing train was allowed into the Absolute Block

section by the section Starting signal and moved towards the next station (or block post), on the approach to which it would pass a Distant signal giving prior warning of the section Home signal ahead.

There are four crucial matters in this process arising from the Requirements that affect the design and operation of any station layout:

1 No train may be allowed into the Absolute Block section unless the line is clear and any facing points set and any other points in their proper positions for a distance of at least a quarter of a mile ahead of the Home signal. This is known as the 'overlap' of the Home signal. If this provision is not met, the signalman cannot accept the train.

2 The train cannot be reported as being out of the Absolute Block section until it is no longer in the overlap of the Home signal and the signalman has seen its tail lamp pass, or been reliably informed that the train has arrived complete, for example if it has gone into a siding.

3 If in the course of shunting it is necessary for an engine or train to move into the overlap of the Home signal, the 'Blocking Back Inside Home Signal' bell signal must be sent and the Absolute Block section treated as occupied. Similarly, if the shunting move is to pass the Home signal, the 'Blocking Back Outside Home Signal' must be sent and the section treated as occupied.

4 If in the course of shunting it is necessary for an engine or train to pass the section Starting signal, the 'Shunting Into Forward Section' signal must be sent and the section treated as occupied. (This is only possible at stations where specific authority has been given.)

Station yard and Permissive working

'Station yard working' is the description used for engine movements within 'station limits', ie the section of line between the Home signal (or Inner Home if there is more than one Home signal) and the Starting or Advanced Starting signal. In other words, a station yard is an area under the direct control of a signalman and not part of the section or block.

Permissive working applies when there is more than one train (in this sense a light engine is also a train) in a section. It is commonly found at large stations where it is controlled by the Local Instructions that apply to that particular place or on certain goods lines as described previously in Chapter 2.

From time to time the expressions 'in rear of' and 'in advance of' have been used, and they require an explanation. These terms are always expressed from the viewpoint of an engine driver moving in the proper direction, but modellers rarely use them; similarly stipulations 1 and 2 above are crucial operational matters, but they are seldom taken account of in the design and operation of model railways. Probably the most common form of model layout is a small branch terminus, where no other train can be accepted, never mind approach, until the arrival platform is clear. Any train occupying that platform must be shunted clear before any new train

is accepted from the station 'in rear'. We may not use bell codes and we can distort time, but if we have modelled the station accurately we are stuck with the way that it is capable of being operated. This may well make the station more interesting to operate, or alternatively the option is open to us, as on the prototype, to add more signals or track to allow us to do everything we want.

For example, we could provide an Outer Home signal at least a quarter of a mile (subject to selective compression for modellers) in rear of the Home, or provide an Advance Starter as far as necessary in advance of the station to allow shunting to start again after the departure of a train into the section ahead. We could provide a safety siding at a junction to allow two trains to approach without them sharing the same overlap. On a small layout these features could be considered as being 'offstage', but if the modeller states that they exist it will enable him to explain why his single-line branch is able to operate a more intensive service than otherwise. At certain stations the Warning Arrangement, or 'Section Clear But Station Or Junction Blocked' signal, allowed trains to approach with limited or no overlap, but this was an unusual situation requiring specific authority.

Once continuous colour light signalling was introduced the overlap was reduced to 200 yards, and further reduced proportionally for lower speeds. Put simply, a signal that is required to stop a train that has been allowed to run at line speed cannot also be used to protect any other movement by just the thickness of the signal post. The Requirements give no specific numbers for Home and Starting signals, but under the Signalling Regulations a block post with just one Stop signal would be awkward to work. A junction might be signalled that way, on the assumption that trains would normally be telegraphed right through, a procedure known as 'double blocking'. The relaxations for light railways state that Distant signals are only required if Stop signals cannot be see for a distance of a quarter of a mile.

Working of single lines

Although there were many miles of single-line railway in Great Britain, the total volume of traffic carried over them was small when compared with the volume on the multi-track lines. It could be said that the single lines were not important in the overall scheme of things, and certainly the closures that took place during the 1960s tend to support this view. Fortunately modellers have ignored this aspect of railway history and in model form single lines flourish. As an observer at exhibitions it seems that at times the volume of traffic and frequency of trains on some of them is a little unrealistic. Therefore in order set out as clearly as possible how they were worked during the steam age I have decided to devote rather more space to single lines than their role in the full-size railway might warrant.

During the period covered by this book, on a double line of railway it was the rule in British practice that, except in the case of emergency, each line should be used exclusively for traffic in one direction. When, on account of the blocking of one road by reason of mishap or if traffic was disrupted by repairs or re-laying, it became necessary to work the traffic in both directions over the other road, the most stringent precautions were taken to avoid two trains meeting on the single line. Until recent years the use of one line of a double-line railway for traffic in both directions was regarded as a wholly abnormal condition of working, but now bi-directional working is commonplace. In ordinary working during the steam era it happened only within station limits or station yards, where setting back in the wrong direction was permitted for limited distances and under local instructions, which set out what was allowed.

There was, however, a considerable mileage of railway consisting of a single line and on these lines arrangements were made for working the traffic in both directions. A method of single-line working known as the 'crossing order' system was employed prior to the passing of the Regulation of Railways Act of 1889. Under this system, when it became necessary for trains to cross one another at a point other than that appointed for them in the timetable, telegraphic instructions were sent from some central point, and the receipt of such instructions by the trainmen and station staffs formed the necessary authority for the regular crossing place to be changed. In the absence of such authority the trainmen were required to satisfy themselves, at each crossing place, that the appointed train or trains from the opposite direction had arrived or passed before they entered the next section of single line. As a rule the use of the crossing order system in this country was supplemented by the block telegraph.

After 1889 three systems were authorised, and I will begin with the Ordinary Train Staff system. The others – which were both based on the principle that the same object cannot be in more than one place at the same time, and that object was the sole authority for a driver to enter a section of single line – were the Train Staff and Ticket system and the Electric Staff or Tablet system. The first and third systems provide security against trains overtaking as well as meeting a train coming from the opposite direction, but the second does not protect against overtaking and has to be supplemented by the block telegraph system.

Single lines may consist either of a separate length of single line, without any intermediate crossing place, or of a line that has a series of lengths of single line separated from one another by short lengths of double line, forming crossing loops. Single lines can range from short branch lines to long cross-country routes.

The Ordinary Train Staff system

The Ordinary Train Staff system can be used only for working lengths of single line over which a train works backwards and forwards alternately, and in practice this happens chiefly on short branch lines with a shuttle service. A wooden staff about 2 feet long, and lettered with the name of the section, is provided, and the possession of this staff is the sole authority for a driver to enter the single line. As the staff can be in the possession of only one driver at a time, it follows that at any time only one engine can be on the single line to which it applies. The regulations for working single lines by Ordinary Train Staff allowed two engines on the line, but they had to remain coupled together during the whole time they remained on the single

line; this system of working was referred to as 'by ordinary train staff with only one engine in steam or two engines coupled together'. This system has continued to be used and is now known as 'One Train Working'.

The Train Staff and Ticket system

If it is necessary to allow more than one train to pass over the single-line section consecutively in the same direction, the train staff alone is not suitable because arrangements would have to be made to return the train staff for the use of the second train. In order to overcome this problem the Staff and Ticket system is used. At the staff stations at either end of the section specially printed coloured tickets are provided, and kept in a box locked with a spring lock. If more than one train has to pass through the section in the same direction before one passes in the opposite direction, the driver of each such train except the last is merely shown the staff and is given a ticket, which is his authority to travel through the section on the strength of having seen the staff. The tickets give authority for a movement in one direction only and cannot be used for an opposite movement. The last train of the series takes the staff, and when it is deposited at the other end of the section it is available for an opposite movement and can be used if required in connection with the tickets kept at that end, which are, of course, also distinctively lettered.

The boxes containing the tickets are unlocked by a key that forms part of the staff itself, and the staff cannot be withdrawn from the lock until the box has been closed and fastened. Provided that the man in charge does not take out more than one ticket at a time, and provided that the enginemen insist on seeing the staff when a ticket is presented to them (which they were required to do), the system was safe. However, it was not an ideal system if the traffic was irregular, because the staff might end up at the 'wrong end' of the section and there would be delays while a messenger was sent to collect it. Furthermore, when a train has entered the section with a ticket there is nothing to prevent another train following immediately with another ticket or with the staff itself. Therefore in order to maintain the space interval between trains ordinary block working was used. On each section of single line worked by train staff, the staff was clearly lettered with the name of the section to which it applied, and it was not unusual for them to be different colours and shapes in order to avoid them being used for the wrong section. A responsible person was authorised to issue the tickets, often the Station Master. The system remained in use after the end of steam traction and was replaced by the Electric Tablet or Token system.

The Electric Tablet and Train Staff systems

These two systems are identical in principle. The tablet is a disc of metal about 6 inches in diameter, and the electric staff is a metal staff similar to an ordinary staff. The Electric Tablet system was the first of the two to be introduced, and its principles were afterwards adapted to an arrangement whereby the

more familiar staff was employed in place of the tablet. In order to facilitate the handling of the tablets, and also to avoid the risk of their being mislaid, they are placed in a leather pouch before being handed to the driver. The pouch has a large loop-shaped handle, which facilitates exchange of tablets while a train is travelling and is used to hang the pouch on a hook in the engine cab. The electric staff is usually handled directly. Various kinds of apparatus have been introduced to enable the staffs to be exchanged at speed. The tablets and the staffs are, like the ordinary train staffs, lettered with the name of the section to which they apply. The methods of working are the same, whether tablet or electric staff, so in the following description the word 'staff' also applies to 'tablet'.

On the single-line section A to B, there is an instrument at A and a similar one at B, and in the two instruments together there is a certain number – say 20 – of staffs. The two instruments are electrically interlocked with one another so that when a staff is withdrawn from either instrument, a second one cannot be withdrawn either from the same instrument or from that at the opposite end of the section until the staff has been replaced in either of the two instruments. Thus if a staff has been withdrawn for a train that is to proceed from A to B, no second staff for that section can be withdrawn until either the train has arrived at B and the staff has been placed in the instrument there, or (should the train not be going forward as intended) until the staff has been replaced in the instrument at A. It will therefore be clearly seen that, as a driver may not enter the single line without

Above right: These three pictures show the hand-over of 'the authority to the driver to be on a single line'. The first was taken from a carriage window of a SLS rail tour and shows how it was often possible for the driver to hand over the staff to the signalman without the signalman leaving his box. *Author's collection*

Far right: This picture, taken in April 1955 at Delph Junction, shows another exchange where the signalman remains in his box. At some signal boxes fixed steps were erected on which the signalman could stand when the exchange was made. *Brian Hilton*

Right: When the signal box was on the opposite side of the line to the train, the signalman would have to leave his box and, depending upon the circumstances, would stand where a clean hand-over could be made. This picture was taken at Cynghordy on the former LNWR Central Wales line in August 1963 and shows an exchange about to take place. The engineman is about to give the signalman the staff, which is attached to a hoop, and the signalman is ready to hand over the staff for the next section. There was a degree of skill involved in this manoeuvre: when I was working on the Evesham branch (see the References) my driver made it very clear to me that I must make sure I got the token (it was in a leather pouch similar to one seen in this picture) and must throw the other on to the ground, trying not to hit the signalman. *D. F. Tee*

a staff, the system affords protection against trains meeting in the section and also against trains overtaking. It is, in fact, a block system, and is more efficient than the block system ordinarily employed on double lines.

The standard block regulations and codes are adapted to the Electric Staff and Tablet systems, and vary only so far as is necessary from the fact of the line being single instead of double. Arrangements are made whereby, should the unequal flow of traffic in one direction cause the staffs to accumulate at one end of the section, the number may be equalised by the lineman, who, under stringent precautions, unlocks the instrument and transfers the necessary number of staffs to the instrument at the opposite end of the section. This system enables single lines to be used to their fullest possible capacity, and at the same time gives perfect security.

Block working without train staff

A variation of single-line working was when block instruments controlled trains and a train staff was not employed. The Great Western, Caledonian, North British, Highland and Great North of Scotland railways all used this method. Later developments in the control of single lines include the use of track circuits, a system known as the 'tokenless block'. Another method to be developed was the 'Radio Electronic Token Block', but to go further would take this subject well beyond the end of the steam era.

Pilot Guard

The final method of single-line working is one that is rarely mentioned, namely by Pilot Guard – whom we must not confuse with a Pilotman, who was usually employed at times of emergency when single-line working over a double-track section of railway was required, as a result of an accident that closed one line or engineering works, such as track re-laying. When this happened a Pilotman had to accompany each

train, or, if there were several trains travelling in the same direction, he would issue the driver with a ticket and travel on the last train, repeating the process in the reverse direction.

A Pilot Guard was different. My own experience of one was on the Kingsbury branch, which was about 5 miles in length and served a number of collieries. The Pilot Guard wore an armband lettered 'Pilot Guard Kingsbury Branch', and his possession of the staff, which he had to show to every driver, authorised all movements on the branch. The sequence began with trains of empty wagons being despatched by him from the branch siding, which was were where the branch joined the main line, and he travelled to the collieries on the last train. When the trains of loaded coal wagons were ready to depart back to the branch sidings, he authorised their departure, returning on the final working. This simplified description should provide readers with an idea of how this form of single-line working was conducted. The branch was a fascinating length of line and could provide the basis for a model of a colliery branch; it had no signals beyond the branch sidings. A full description of the line will be found in *British Railway Journal* (see the References).

Signalling on single lines

At all staff or tablet stations on single lines – ie at each place at the end of a section to which a staff applies – it is obvious that (so far as the staff working is concerned) there may be more than one train present or approaching at the same time. Hence all such places must have a full complement of signals, and these must be provided in accordance with exactly the same principles that apply on an ordinary double line. This is the case if the single line is worked by any of the three systems, with the exception that signals are unnecessary at the terminal end of a single-line branch on which only one engine in steam is allowed at a time and which is, therefore, worked by an Ordinary Train Staff without tickets. Although such a station is actually a staff station, no second engine can possibly approach when one is already there, so the necessity

Below: To enlarge upon my comments in the text about Pilot Guards, this diagram shows the sidings at Kingsbury, and although the junction of the branch was with a busy main line, this should not deter modellers; colliery lines also connected with single lines that carried sparse passenger traffic, so the entire layout could be simplified considerably while retaining the essential features. A main line, of one or two tracks, is needed, together with the means to move from the main line to the branch and vice versa. Note that entering the branch from either the up or down line can only be made in the trailing direction, so the train has to set back.

At Kingsbury most of the empty wagons for the colliery came from Birmingham and the loaded wagons went towards Birmingham. The empty wagon trains ran along the up main line until the brake-van was by the signal box; the points were then reversed and the train set back on to the down main line until the locomotive was clear of the trailing points that connected the down main with the branch. When these were set, the train drew forward on to the branch, now under the control of the Pilot Guard.

If space was not available the traffic sidings at the Birmingham end of the layout could be dispensed with and only the branch sidings retained. The drawing shows two fans of sidings: my recollection is that one was used to hold loaded wagons that would be worked away by the same engines that brought the empty wagons, while the other was used to hold empty wagons that were to be taken to the collieries. If space is restricted these sidings could be reduced to two, one for loads and the other for empties. Note the shunter's cabin on the right and the Stop signal, which was controlled by the shunters. It was a self-contained railway that was run by the Pilot Guard, and once a train was on the branch it was out of the main-line signalman's control. I have always felt that a model based upon Kingsbury would be fascinating.

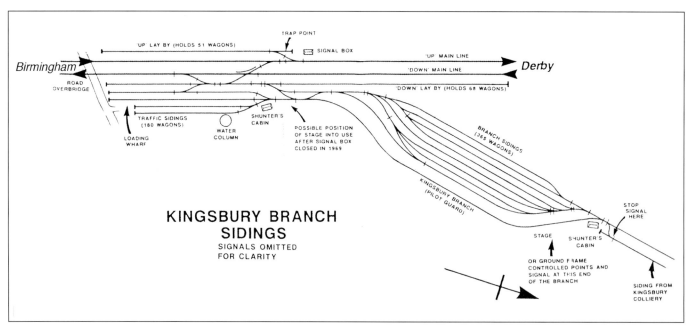

KINGSBURY BRANCH
SIDINGS
SIGNALS OMITTED
FOR CLARITY

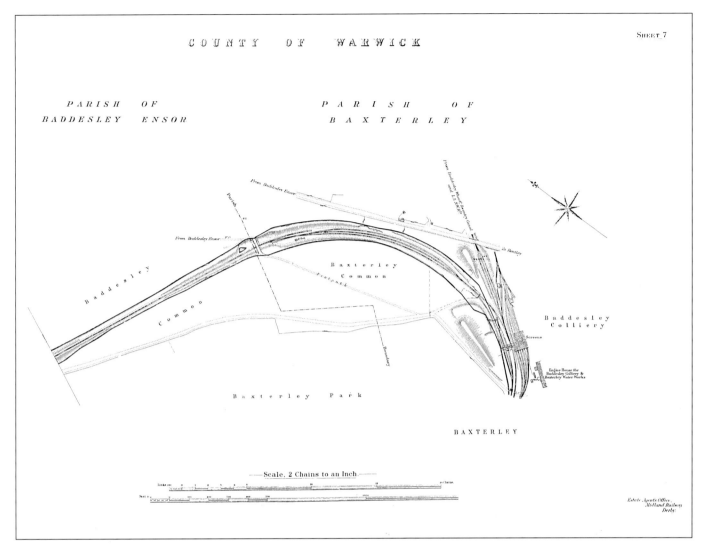

Above: This plan provides readers with details of an interesting layout for a colliery that could be adapted for model purposes. Baddesley Colliery was at the end of the colliery branch from Kingsbury. It was not unusual for more than one railway company engine to be at the colliery, and the Pilot Guard controlled all the movements. Note the two sidings that ran parallel with the branch just before the gates that marked the end of the railway company track and the start of the colliery's private sidings. There was also a short siding that would hold a locomotive and brake-van. The arrangement of the sidings meant that two trains could be held and still leave an empty line for other engine movements. The colliery was also connected to the LNWR and the Coventry Canal, while the incomplete bottom of the map shows colliery lines crossing a road and presumably continuing to additional colliery-owned sidings.

for signals disappears unless a level crossing is involved.

The conditions under which trains may be allowed to approach a block or staff post on a single line are also the same as those applying on double lines, with one exception. Usually, but not invariably, there is a passing loop at a staff station. As it is necessary for two trains that have to cross one another to approach the loop simultaneously, it is clearly impossible to provide for the usual quarter-mile clearance. Trains are therefore allowed to approach provided the line is clear up to the signal at the end of the loop line into which each is to run. The signals at the entrance to the loop are kept at danger, and the train arriving first is admitted first; when it has come to a stand in the loop line and is clear of the opposite loop, the train from the opposite direction is allowed to enter. If there is no crossing loop at a staff post two trains are not allowed to approach simultaneously when strict block working is in force.

Locking of intermediate siding connections

At all staff stations on single lines there must necessarily be a complete set of running signals. When a connection leading to a siding occurs at an intermediate point within a staff section, the conditions are different. A train within the section, which is of course in possession of the staff, is master of the situation and no other train can approach it from either direction. Hence any shunting at an intermediate siding is perfectly safe and no signals are required to protect the operation. There is, however,

still the necessity to ensure that, when the siding is not in use, the points (which, it must be remembered, will be facing points in one direction) are lying securely for the main line and that the siding catch points are protecting the main line from any vehicles that might be pushed along the siding.

This security is very simply obtained by locking the lever working the siding points by means of the train staff. For this purpose the train staff (if there is only one), or each staff (in the case of the Electric Staff system), is fitted with a key. In the case of the Tablet system the tablet itself is placed in a slide in the siding lever frame and acts as a key. Until the staff key or tablet is thus inserted in the lever frame, the lever cannot be moved, and when the lever has once been moved for the purpose of working the points the staff or tablet cannot be withdrawn. Thus the possession by a driver of the staff or tablet when arriving at the end of the section forms a mechanical assurance that the points of the intermediate siding have been left in the proper position for the main line, and there is no risk of the trainmen having inadvertently left the points in the wrong position.. In practice the locking takes place in connection with the lever working the facing point lock.

It is obvious that this arrangement cannot be employed at junctions where a train may have to leave the direct route altogether, or, under ordinary circumstances, at points at which trains have to be shunted for others to pass, as under such circumstances, after the train had been placed clear of the main line, the staff would have to be taken by hand to the nearest staff station. It should be added, however, that supplementary apparatus has been devised whereby the shunting of trains on single lines at other than staff stations can be effected, but we do not need to go into these while discussing first principles.

On single lines worked by the Staff and Ticket system, intermediate siding points, if locked by the staff, are again perfectly safe and no signals are necessary, but of course the siding could not then be used by a train carrying a ticket. Hence it is usual when this system is employed to equip an intermediate siding with signals in both directions instead of locking them by the staff, so that a train with a ticket may use it with suitable protection should a following train find its way into the section by mistake. If it is desired to shunt trains for others to pass at such places, they should be equipped as block telegraph posts. However, the expense involved in thus equipping intermediate sidings, and the measure of risk involved by such signals not being in regular use for each train, are among the strongest reasons in favour of equipping a single line with the Electric Staff or Tablet system, thus enabling signals at intermediate sidings to be dispensed with entirely.

The circumstances under which signals can be dispensed with on single lines may be summarised thus. Signals are not required at any intermediate siding within a section worked by ordinary staff, electric staff or tablet when the staff or tablet locks the points. If a staff and tickets are in use, signals are necessary unless it can be arranged that trains requiring to call at the siding always carry the staff, and that the staff unlocks the points. Signals are not necessary at the terminal stations of lines on which only one engine in steam, or two coupled together, are allowed at a time. If, however, more than one engine is allowed on the line, signals must be provided whether the working is by the Ordinary Train Staff and Ticket or Electric Staff or Tablet systems. Under all other circumstances, a full equipment of signals is necessary.

Gradients on single lines

On a single line it is obviously impossible to guard against the risk of vehicles running back on inclines by providing catch points, as such points would derail traffic proceeding correctly in the other direction. The possibility of trains breaking away after having come to a stand at a Home signal or while surmounting a brow or upon a change of gradient during passage through a section cannot therefore be dealt with as on double lines.

If a crossing loop occurs on a gradient the risk of vehicles within the loop running back on to the single line is prevented by providing a catch point worked from the signal box just clear of the converging point of the two loop lines. As the risk of a breakaway is greatest at places at which trains have necessarily to be brought to a stand, the Board of Trade does not allow a station or a siding connection on a single line where the gradient is steeper than 1 in 260, unless certain precautions are taken against the risk of vehicles running back indefinitely on the single line.

If it is necessary to erect a station on such a gradient, it must be formed as a double-line station, catch points being provided at the lower end of the loop as explained above. If circumstances render this arrangement impossible, a loop line with a catch point must be provided lower down the incline. In this case the facing points would have to remain set for the ascending loop line, so that in the event of vehicles running back from the station they would be diverted into this loop and become derailed at the catch points at the lower end. The loop would, of course, have to be properly signalled. It should be added that this alternative method is very seldom resorted to in the case of stations on gradients.

In the case of a siding connection on a gradient, there must either be a loop, as in the case of a station, in order that a train having to call at the siding may be left standing on the loop and within the catch points when the engine is detached, or, failing this, either of two other methods must be adopted: there must be sufficient room inside the sidings for the whole train to be placed there, clear of the main line, before the engine is detached for shunting operations, or there must be an engine at the lower end of a train calling at the siding. In most cases, the latter would be found an inconvenient method, although the railway companies gave undertakings to this effect to the Board of Trade.

Appendix 1 may be anticipated here so far as to explain that the Board of Trade regulations in respect of the arrangement and working of stations and siding connections on inclines apply only to such cases that had been brought into use since the requirement was first laid down. The Board of Trade had no power to order these arrangements at existing places that it may not have had occasion to inspect since then.

In concluding this chapter it may be mentioned that the methods adopted in the working of single lines offer a wide field for investigation. Many very interesting variations, for example in the Electric Staff and Tablet systems, have been introduced to meet various contingencies. Some are in use in this country, while others were adapted to the conditions prevailing abroad where standards of safety were less exacting. Operating single lines in model form offers many opportunities for creative modelling and I look forward to seeing how modellers react to the challenge.

Below: I have described the arrangements for catch points on single lines in the text but I felt that I should illustrate a catch point on a double line where there is a tunnel. Haw Bank tunnel was 218 yards long and it was between Skipton and Embsay Junction on the Skipton & Ilkley branch. The gradient, clearly seen in this *c*1952 picture, was 1 in 90. Note the tunnel nameboard, which also gave the length in yards. *D. Ibbotson*

Chapter Four

Signal Stations

I must begin by making it quite clear that the term 'signal stations' does not, as far as I am aware, have any official basis. I have used it for this chapter to embrace all forms of signalling control installations, the most obvious being the signal box, although there were other places where signalling equipment was to be found. For example, some stations did not have a signal box, but simply a lever frame on the platform and the instruments close by or in an office. An independent ground frame was another place where levers operated points and, maybe, a shunting signal, but generally the 'signalling' was by hand. It therefore seemed logical to bring into one chapter examples of the various places where signalling and point operation took place, and to begin with the Requirements.

The Requirements state that, for economy and avoidance of confusion, the number of signals and their height should be limited to what is actually necessary. Taken to its logical conclusion, this could mean that any movements other than those associated with block working could be controlled by verbal instructions, flags and lamps. This would be acceptable provided that all movements could be so controlled without any confusion arising from the engine being too far away, or the view being obstructed by an underbridge, or being required too frequently. Certainly this arrangement was normal for 'one engine in steam' operation, or indeed at any place where the points were locked by the staff or token; it was also allowed in the relaxations that applied to light railways.

The Requirements state that a signal box should be positioned and constructed so that the signalman should be able to see all the Stop signals it controls, and these and all other signals should also have backlights visible at night if their front lights cannot be seen from the signal box. Any signals that cannot be seen, as well as Distant signals, are to be repeated on instruments in the signal box. At those locations where shunting requires 'blocking back' or 'shunt ahead', the limit of such shunting movements should be indicated by an illuminated sign. With mechanical signalling from a conventional lever frame, the signal box must be sited and the frame fitted to give the signalman the best possible view of the operations for which he is responsible. The distance limit for levers from mechanically worked points was 150 yards until 1892, 180 yards for facing and 300 yards for trailing points until 1925, and 350 yards thereafter. Power-worked points could be at any distance provided occupation of the lines is indicated by track circuits; from 1925 track circuit diagrams became acceptable if a view was not possible. Detector bars are to be provided to define the fouling points of junctions and other points where it may be difficult for a signalman to estimate clearance.

One of the first and greatest concerns of the Board of Trade inspectors was the safety of trains moving over points. Everything needed was already in the 1858 Requirements, and continues with minor modifications to the present day. The key elements are:

1 There must be locks on all facing points used by passenger trains and detection with relevant signals to prevent signals being pulled off if the points are not set and locked.
2 Locking bars, longer than the greatest distance between two axles, must be fitted to prevent facing points being moved under passing trains.
3 Points must be interlocked to prevent conflicting routes being set, and there must be interlocking of signals with points and locks, and detection of signals with trailing points.
4 The number of facing points must be kept to a minimum, and positioned as close to the box as possible; this ceased to be a requirement in 1925 due to the development of point motors.
5 Reminder apparatus, eg detector bars, must be provided for standing vehicles at platforms that are already occupied. If electrical, the apparatus must lock the relevant signals.

There is further reference to detection and fouling bars in Chapter 3.

Development of signal boxes

'Block post', 'signal cabin' or 'signal box' – all these descriptions were used on the full-size railway and they will appear in this book, as they all have the same meaning. The present signal box began as a form of 'sentry box' for the policeman who was responsible for regulating the traffic; he would leave his box to go to the points and signals in order to work the necessary levers. The next step was to concentrate the levers in one place in order to avoid the policeman having to move around the layout. It was therefore a logical step to provide a shelter or 'cabin' for both the policeman and his equipment, which was obviously a definite requirement once interlocking and telegraphy was introduced.

At first signal boxes were at ground level, but it was soon realised that the signalman would have a better view if the cabin was raised above rail level. The next step was the introduction of the telegraph system, and by the 1850s the earliest form of what today we call a signal box had arrived, although it was not until the mid-1870s, with the development of the block telegraph, that the construction of signal boxes began in earnest.

The first signal boxes were generally small, but as traffic increased and more points and signals were installed, so the size of the lever frame and signal box increased. Only a few companies used their own designs of signalling equipment, most preferring to use 'the trade,' or signal contractors as they were generally known. The subject of the design and size of individual company signal boxes is complex, and readers wishing to explore the subject are referred to the References in Appendix 2.

The first power signalling installation was brought into use in Great Britain in 1899, and while the use of power increased the distance at which a set of points could be worked from the signal box, in general it did not reduce the number of signal boxes required until much later. The signals were still the semaphore type,

Right: Sutton West box on the old London, Brighton & South Coast Railway was photographed in about 1955 and is an example of a wooden-built signal box. The small building to the left was probably the closet. *Lens of Sutton*

A selection of signal boxes

This selection of signal boxes with brief captions is intended to give readers an idea of something of the rich variety of designs that could be seen in Great Britain during the later days of steam. It is far from comprehensive, while space does not permit details of the number of levers in each frame. Note also that, just as a particular railway company's locomotives and carriages were identifiable, to a large degree the same applied to its signal boxes and signals. The signal boxes are identified by their pre-Grouping owners, even though some may have been constructed after 1923.

Left: Audley End Junction is seen in 1954, looking towards Bishops Stortford on the former Great Eastern Railway. It is a fairly tall timber-built box, and of interest is the banner repeating signal on the gantry to the right. *Lens of Sutton*

Below: Kiveton Park Colliery signal box was on the Great Central Railway line between Sheffield and Lincoln, not far from Retford. Again built entirely of wood, it presents a rather austere appearance. Note the large wooden coal bunkers. *H. B. Priestley*

Right: The South Yorkshire Joint Railway was owned by the Great Central, Great Northern, Lancashire & Yorkshire, Midland and North Eastern companies. This 1959 view shows the wooden signal box at Tickhill & Wadworth. The coal bunker is close to the foot of the steps. *H. B. Priestley*

Below right: Beamish was on the North Eastern Railway, and when this picture of the signal box was taken in 1965 the station had been closed and largely demolished. *R. S. Carpenter*

Above: The old London & South Western Railway signal box at the rear of the platform at Cobham has a brick base with a timber cabin. While I cannot be certain, I doubt if there are more than 16 levers in the frame. *Lens of Sutton*

Right: Branksome signal box, near Bournemouth, was another LSWR structure, and again I expect the number of levers did not exceed 16. Of pleasing design, this is the size of signal box that will appeal to many modellers. *Lens of Sutton*

Left: Hothfield is between Maidstone and Ashford on the former South Eastern & Chatham line, and this signal box, described on the nameboard as 'Hothfield Signals', is another example of a brick base and timber construction. Note also a good example of a Southern lattice-post upper-quadrant signal in this circa 1960 picture. *Lens of Sutton*

Left: The old brick-built LB&SCR signal box at Petworth was photographed in the 1950s. There appear to be 16 levers in the frame. *Lens of Sutton*

Right: Sleaford East is an old Great Northern Railway signal box, and this circa 1970 view shows a brick base and rear wall with a timber window section. *R. S. Carpenter collection*

Below: The Mound was the junction for the Highland Railway's Dornoch branch. This 1952 picture shows the similarly constructed brick signal box at the station. *R. S. Carpenter collection*

Left: Carnwath signal box, seen here in 1951, was on the former Caledonian Railway line between Edinburgh and Carstairs, and is interesting if only for the rock garden at the foot of the stairs. Gardens on stations were quite common, but generally they were on the platform well away from the signal box. *R. S. Carpenter collection*

Below left: In contrast to the majority of signal box pictures in this chapter, which were photographed during the British Railways period, this picture of the brick-built Great Western cabin at Widney Manor, on the main line from Birmingham to Leamington Spa, was photographed in about 1907. *Lens of Sutton*

Above right: It was not uncommon to place a signal box directly on the platform. This picture shows Faygate on the old LB&SCR Horsham to Three Bridges line in the early 1960s. *Lens of Sutton*

Below: The signal box at the Midland Railway's Cheltenham Lansdown station, seen here in 1960, was rather squat; no steps were needed, as entry was direct from the platform. *Author's collection*

99

Left: This elevated signal box was photographed at Epsom, LSWR, in the late 1950s. A number of similar boxes, built on elevated steel structures, could be seen around the country. The reasons varied from the need to provide a good view for the signalman to problems with the site, when this method of construction presented the best solution. Whatever the reason, one would make a very impressive model. Note what appears to be the closet at the top of the steps. *Lens of Sutton*

Above: The Great Western Railway signal box at Norton Fitzwarren Junction, seen in this 1964 picture, was rather large – perhaps too big for the majority of modellers. *R. S. Carpenter*

Left: Another large GWR box was that at Yatton West, which was an impressive brick structure, as seen in this 1961 picture. *R. S. Carpenter*

which, although power-worked, still had to be seen to have operated and that the lamps were lit. The number of signal boxes could not be reduced until track circuiting was proved reliable and colour light signalling installed.

While London's underground railways led the way with the Baker Street installation in 1913, it was the Liverpool Overhead Railway that pioneered the use of daylight colour light signals in 1921. Track circuits occupied by a train could easily be repeated on an illuminated diagram within the signal box, as could the signal indications; it follows therefore that the signalman no longer needed to see the actual train or the signals, which meant that one signal box could control many miles of railway. The tail lamp no longer required to be observed, as should the train break into two portions the track circuit would hold the appropriate signals at danger and the track would be shown as occupied on the signal box diagram. A disadvantage of power signalling was that the signalman could no longer check the train for open doors or axle boxes running hot, etc.

From the 1930s the developments that were to lead to the modern system were under way and credit for this must go to the LNER for the route/relay interlocking signal box opened at Thirsk in 1933. The interlocking was performed by electrical relays and route setting by thumb switches. The scheme was known as the 'One Control Switch', or OCS, system, and was later adopted by British Railways in the late 1940s and 1950s.

If I may digress slightly, based upon my own experience with the Dewsbury layout, this is the way forward. Dewsbury has two lever frames, one with 24 levers and the other with 18. Both are mechanically interlocked and the design and construction of the frames was a task that required the talents of two modellers who were far more able than me, whereas the ability to construct electrical interlocking by using relays and switches is probably more widely understood.

Signal box size and construction

One of the most common faults found on model railways is that the signal box does not suit the layout. For example, a simple single-line terminus may have a signal box that is too large, the reason perhaps being that the modeller has used a kit and 'a signal box is a signal box'. Not so – size is important.

The basis for deciding upon the size of signal box was the number of levers it would require in full-size practice. For example, the original Dewsbury Station Junction signal box on my layout had a 16-lever frame with each lever in use, but the alterations made subsequently to the layout involved additional points and signals that, in full-size practice, would have required a 24-lever frame. Since the size of the model signal box was too small for a 24-lever frame, it had to be replaced with a larger box. In this respect the model followed full-size practice. However, should there be a reduction in the number of levers in use, this would not mean that the signal box was replaced by a smaller building. What would probably happen is that the frame would be left in the box and there would be several levers described

as 'spare', and painted white, the usual colour for levers that were not in use. One feature of full-size practice was that, generally on the more important lines, as more levers were introduced in order to control the more complex layout, the size of signal boxes increased.

During the 1930s in particular, cost-saving programmes saw the closure of one of a pair of signal boxes with the remaining box being either enlarged or replaced by a larger structure. This meant that a single box and one signalman on each shift replaced two boxes requiring two men on each shift. Although the manning arrangements on the full-size railway may not be of interest to modellers, the result of these changes in signal box size and position may need to be reflected in a model.

The various pictures included in this chapter will show examples of signal boxes made of wood or brick, or the upper part in wood and the lower part in brick. Stone was also used, but was far less common. The deciding factors were varied: when built on embankments wood was generally used, and this also

Above: This Southern Railway-period picture of Esher illustrates that there were two signal boxes, one at each end of the station – the other can just be seen beyond the distant signal gantry. In such circumstances advancing technology might have made it possible to abolish one of the boxes and concentrate all the functions in the other. Note also the contrast between the lattice-post signal on the left and the old slotted wooden post in the centre. *Author's collection*

applied if the box was on newly made-up or boggy ground where it was difficult to secure a stable foundation. Cost, possible future enlargement and the preferences of the signal engineer also played a part in the final decision. In some cases, due to lack of space or for sighting purposes, some boxes were built over the permanent way; these were usually known as 'overhead boxes', with the Midland, LNWR, NER and some lines in southern England using this method.

Signal box fittings

Over the years the signal box developed from a basic cabin with few facilities to one that catered for all the needs of the signalman, who, unless it was on a line with very little traffic, was obliged to remain in his box. As a result the signalman was provided with a stove or a fireplace, while some had a gas stove for cooking during hot weather when the heating stove was not in use. A coal bunker and an ash bin would be close to the cabin, as can be seen in the accompanying pictures. Closets were also an essential feature, and the position varied: some were fixed at the top of the cabin steps, while others were close to the cabin or in the locking room below. The block instruments were placed over the locking frame on the shelf provided. Some windows opened to allow the signalman to communicate with enginemen and others working outside the box.

The levers themselves were painted in distinctive colours to assist identity. The painting of levers was revised from time to time; for example, the LMS issued an instruction in 1931 only to simplify it in 1934 as follows:

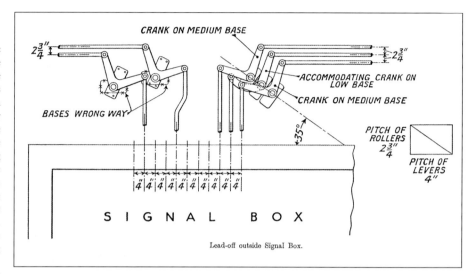

Lead-off outside Signal Box.

Above right: This drawing, reproduced from *Railway Signalling and Communications* (see the References), shows how point rods lead off from the base of a signal box via cranks.

Right: Photographed on the Midland Railway's Settle & Carlisle line in the mid-1960s, this view shows point rods running alongside the running lines. Note also the flat-bottom rail and the disc signal with an arrow indicated the line to which it applies. *Paul Cottrell*

Below: This pre-Great War picture of the Midland Railway at St Pancras shows a number of interesting features, including the round rods used to work the points and the various rollers. Note also the signal wires, wheels and chains together with the wooden boards covering some of the mechanism. *Author's collection*

Black   Points; points and bar; points and bar
         and/or lock; points and point indicator;
         scotch or derailer
Blue   Bolts and/or bars, all types
Red   Signals, running or shunt, other than
         Distant signals
Yellow   Distant signals
Brown   Wicket gates, gate stops, gate locks
Green   'Asking' levers; permission levers;
         'king' levers; route and directional levers;
         indicator levers and gong levers
White   Spare levers

Detonator-placer levers were painted with alternate black and white chevrons 4 inches wide; the point of the chevron was upwards for up lines, and downwards for down lines.

Any lever requiring to be released by the action of a person in another box was distinguished by a 4-inch horizontal white bar halfway down the lever.

It should also be noted that any lever that operated electrically (ie one operating motorised signals, points or colour lights) was painted as above but had the lever handles shortened.

For absolute accuracy, it is suggested that the modeller checks the regulations on his favoured line.

Above: This early Edwardian picture of St Pancras shows the Midland design of 'hammerhead' calling-on arm together with the various rods and cranks that were a feature of mechanical signalling.

Below: A selection of signal and hand lamps photographed in 1967 in Garsdale signal box on the Settle & Carlisle line. *Paul Cottrell*

Left: Every signal box had a stove, like this 'LM&SR' example, which during the winter months was continuously alight. Modellers should be aware of the need to ensure that there is a coal store close to the model signal box. *Author's collection*

Below: The timber walkway at the Midland Railway station at Bolton Abbey, seen in this 1907 picture, is rather unusual, but the main reason for including this picture is to draw attention to the disc hanging on the end of the signal box to the right of the door. It is painted blue and is a telegraph fault signboard, indicating that the telegraph equipment is working correctly. If the reverse side, which was painted black, was displayed it would indicate a fault, and if it was hung horizontally with the blue face outward it would mean that the telephone or telegraph was faulty. *Author's collection*

The Prince of Wales at Bolton Abbey Station   Aug 20th '07 "Mercury" Copyt

Right: On single lines 'interlocking frames', controlled by the tablet or train staff, enabled intermediate points to be unlocked and movements from the single line into sidings made. Sometimes these lever frames also controlled shunting signals. This drawing illustrates an example of this type of frame.

Other signal stations

I have mentioned the practice of not having a signal box at a station where the traffic is light, and since this type of layout is more likely to appeal to the average modeller than, say, a 'Paddington' or a 'Waterloo', let us consider the options. The term 'station' is usually associated with passenger traffic, but as stated in the other books in this series goods depots were also referred to as 'stations', and for the purpose of this chapter we will adopt an all-embracing approach to the subject.

If we begin with a single line to a colliery or similar industrial undertaking, worked as 'one engine in steam', then clearly no signals will be needed at the terminus. The only signals required would be to allow the train onto the branch and, on the return journey, to allow the train to rejoin the main-line system. The same would apply if it was a line carrying passenger traffic. On some lines one engine worked both the passenger and freight traffic, and since a second engine was not allowed onto the line no signals were required other than again to permit a train to run onto or leave the branch at the main-line junction.

Some lines carried more traffic. In addition to one engine working a passenger service between the main-line junction and the branch terminus, some workings might also run as mixed trains, conveying both passenger and goods traffic, and there would also be a daily stopping freight train. This would mean that sometimes there would be two engines at the terminus, and in these circumstances some fixed signals would be required, but the temptation to include a signal box should be resisted. On most full-size railways the few levers required would either be in the open on the platform or in a small hut with the instruments close by, maybe in an office. Apart from saving the cost of installing and maintaining a signal box, it meant that the lowest grade of signalman, namely a Porter Signalman, could be employed, and during the intervals between trains he could attend to other duties.

Another form of 'signalling' was from an independent lever frame that was bolt-locked from a signal box. Usually these were on goods lines or at goods stations, but there were exceptions, and ground frames could be found at terminal passenger stations, perhaps when the signal box was too far away from a set of points, or they saved having to enlarge the signal box in the case of track modifications. The shunter or fireman would call the signalman by an electrical bell

Right: The 8-mile-long Midland Railway Grassington branch was worked by electric token, and this *c*1905 picture shows a lever frame similar to that in the accompanying drawing, controlling the crossover between the two platforms. The locomotive is Midland Railway 0-4-4T No 1535, later No 1269. *Author's collection*

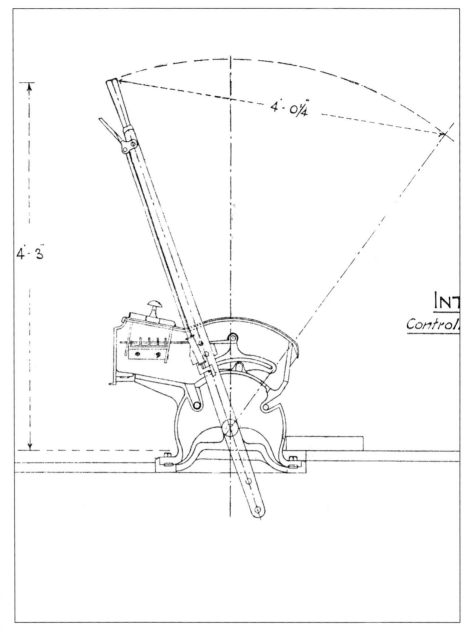

or by telephone and the signalman would unlock the point lever frame to allow the points to be moved. When the engine (and train if it was a movement from a goods line into a goods siding, station or private siding) was clear, the points would be reversed and set to the normal position, allowing the signalman to bolt-lock the frame again. Apart from goods stations, they were usually found at terminal stations and I have included a picture to show an example of how they were installed.

Above: This picture of Longdown station on the GWR branch from Exeter to Heathfield was taken in about 1910 and shows the East Ground Frame with three levers, one controlling the signal, another the point with the third the facing point lock. *Lens of Sutton*

Below: This 1965 picture was taken at Bath Green Park and shows a fairly common arrangement of a local ground frame controlling the points that allowed a locomotive to run round its train. Communication with the signal box varied – it might be by telephone, bell, gong or verbally from a third party on the platform who was in direct touch with the signalman. *Paul Cotterell*

Above: This three-lever frame, also at Bath Green Park in about 1957, appears to have a 'face disc' to the right of the frame. *R. S. Carpenter*

Above right: Although it is not possible to read the name on the diagram behind the levers, this picture is included because it represents a form of 'signal station' that is rarely modelled. Without knowing the location it is impossible to comment other than to say that lever frames controlling both signals and points could be found throughout the British railway system at small stations, and on many model layouts this would be more realistic than a signal box.
Author's collection

Below: On many single lines there were level crossings at places that were not block posts, and this 1966 view of Idridgehay on the Midland Railway's Wirksworth branch is a typical example. The covered ground frame at the end of the platform contains a lever frame working the two signals, which were kept at danger when the gates were open for road traffic and reversed to show 'Clear' when the gates were open for the railway; normally the locking would prevent the signals from showing 'Clear' if the gates were open for the road. Depending upon the circumstances a porter-signalman or gatekeeper would be on duty during the period that trains were running.
D. Ibbotson

Above: The nameboard on the side of the cabin appears to read 'Steen Bridge Ground Frame', on the former Great Western Railway line from Worcester to Leominster, and the levers controlling the facing point lock and the points can be seen in this 1953 view. The point rod on the left probably controls the points at the other end of the crossover. *R. S. Carpenter collection*

Left: This rather delightful picture shows what the photographer describes as a 'board signal' for level crossing protection. It was photographed in 1950 at the Malton Road crossing on the old North Eastern Railway's Pickering to Raskelf branch. Three levers can be seen in the ground frame; I presume that one controls the board, with its lamp that would show either a green or red aspect, and the others control the two Stop signals that would show 'Danger' when the crossing was closed to the railway. *W. S. Garth*

Below: 'Main-line' signal boxes did not have to be large – some were very small, and I offer this picture to show how small they could be. Photographed in 1948, this is the old Lancashire & Yorkshire Railway 'Down Platform Box' at Rochdale. *Author's collection*

Left: Another small signal box is seen on the former Great Western Railway at Felin Fach, on the Aberayron branch. The photograph was taken in 1964. *R. S. Carpenter collection*

Right: I have included this picture of the GWR ground frame at Middleway Bridge Crossing as an example of something rather unusual. Photographed in about 1949, the rodding from the lever frame crosses a small river before being connected to the points. *Author's collection*

Left: A somewhat more conventional ground frame is this Midland Railway example, at Ingrow station on the Worth Valley branch. The black horizontal strip on the reverse of the Distant signal was replaced by a vertical black strip from 1911 onwards. Modellers of the Midland Railway should note that ground frames of this type were still in service at the end of the steam era. *L&GRP*

Chapter Five

A Modeller's Viewpoint

This final chapter comprises a small miscellany of personal recollections that will hopefully be of interest and help to many readers. We will begin with my view of what can be seen at exhibitions. Layouts and their builders' attitudes vary enormously. A layout may be a length of railway running through scenery where a succession of trains can be seen. A variation of this is the vintage layout, some powered by clockwork and others three-rail electric systems, and I enjoy watching the trains run round and round the very sharp curves that were standard with the toy trains of yesteryear. At the other extreme is the layout where the builders have attempted to get as close to prototype practice as possible, and as a result you have realism in miniature. I enjoy the former and relish the latter. In between there are many variations, including layouts under construction, which can be very helpful to the visitor who has not started to build his own model railway and can see and learn how layouts are built. What I do not enjoy are layouts where prototype practice is largely ignored, leaving me wondering why, for example, the signals are fixed in the 'on' or 'off' position and cannot be moved.

When I view a model railway I invariably begin by looking at the permanent way. This and the associated signalling usually tell me most of what I need to know about the builder's understanding of the prototype and therefore his ability to construct a realistic model. Some readers may find this statement rather arrogant, but my feeling is that it is no more than an appraisal of what is on display. The first clue is usually provided by the presence or absence of 'safety points', more commonly described as trap or catch points. On some layouts they are not required, but generally they are, and as we have seen there are clear rules for their use. I have little doubt that many modellers take the view, 'Why spend money on something that is designed to derail my stock?' A valid point, but only if it is not your intention to try and achieve realism in miniature.

I have mentioned the question of length and space, and in my opinion these are the biggest obstacles to be overcome. One solution I have adopted is to model the Edwardian era, when everything on wheels was smaller and therefore you do not need the lengthy trains that were commonplace in the later years of the steam railway. One very constructive idea came from the late John Horton, which was to model the fish bays of Birmingham New Street station. What he proposed to build was just a small part of a large city station, which to a degree was a self-contained unit, and to imagine that the rest of the station was 'offstage'. The idea of building part of a large location, and by means of bridges, other large buildings and high walls to provide a scenic break, has much to commend it.

Over the years some very imaginative prototype plans for layouts have been published, and I would suggest that, providing they are adapted to comply with the Requirements, many could be used to make excellent model railways. If I were to start again I would endeavour to find a real location that could be adapted as a model. If it was to be a small terminal station I would consider an urban rather than a country station on the grounds that they tended to be more compact and cramped, which is what many models are in reality.

On the full-size railway during the steam era communication between drivers and others was by signals rather than verbally. There were exceptions – the signalman might stop an engine as it approached his signal box by using a red flag or light and, with the engine close by, he could speak to the driver, or a driver might stop and either he or his fireman would go to the signal box to see the signalman – but most communications between railwaymen were by signals. We have considered all manner of fixed signals in previous chapters, but I would like to mention hand signals. The accompanying drawings, taken from the LMS 1933 Rule Book, show some of the hand signals that were in use. My friends and I use them when operating, and it makes little difference whether the driver and shunter are 1 foot or 10 feet apart, the meaning is clear. The 'Stop' signal is to show the face of the palm towards the driver. The 'Slow down' signal, most useful when the driver is approaching stock that has to be coupled to his engine, is to move the fingers of one hand up and down. The 'Right away' signal is a variation of what is shown – I found that many railwaymen gave this signal by waving their hand, rather like waving goodbye, but my version is to gently move the palm of the hand from side to side. The 'Move away from' hand signal is to rotate the forefinger in a circle, and the 'Move towards' hand signal is to beckon with the fingers. There is no need to speak and certainly no need to use headphones or similar electronic equipment if you wish to savour the steam era in model form.

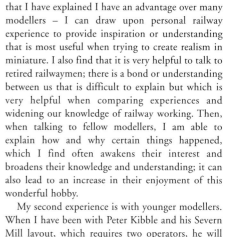

I will conclude with two personal experiences, the first of which is about adult modellers. For reasons that I have explained I have an advantage over many modellers – I can draw upon personal railway experience to provide inspiration or understanding that is most useful when trying to create realism in miniature. I also find that it is very helpful to talk to retired railwaymen; there is a bond or understanding between us that is difficult to explain but which is very helpful when comparing experiences and widening our knowledge of railway working. Then, when talking to fellow modellers, I am able to explain how and why certain things happened, which I find often awakens their interest and broadens their knowledge and understanding; it can also lead to an increase in their enjoyment of this wonderful hobby.

My second experience is with younger modellers. When I have been with Peter Kibble and his Severn Mill layout, which requires two operators, he will often invite youngsters to try their hand on the control panel. He begins by asking the accompanying adult if he can ask the boy – there has never been a girl! – if he would like to operate his layout. With approval given, he speaks to the youngster and asks if he has a train set. Invariably the answer is 'Yes', so Peter invites them to come and play with his. The look on the boy's face is wonderful, and he comes to the control panel where we carefully explain the controls and what we are doing. I find that once the lad overcomes the tendency to run trains too quickly, he soon grasps how the controls work, usually more quickly than an adult, and more than once he has begun to tell us what he is doing and why. The lesson to be learned is simply this – youngsters will respond to guidance and are very quick to learn. It does not matter that the railway is a model of the Edwardian era and modern diesels or electric trains are not part of the scene. These experiences have shown me that we need to encourage the younger generation to become involved in the hobby, and that they quickly understand complex operating moves.

I hope that this and the three preceding volumes have been helpful to my fellow modellers in improving their understanding of how the traditional steam railway was operated, and have provided some ideas that will help them to reproduce it in model form. If this proves to be the case then the time and effort expended over the past few years will have been worthwhile.

Left: I am rather proud of this section of track. It was built in 1989 to prove to myself that Scale 7 was a workable proposition, and is a single slip between the up and down main lines on my Dewsbury layout. The picture was taken shortly after the track was proved and since then, apart from one stretcher rod that became unsoldered, I have never had any problems with it.

HAND SIGNALS

(b) Either arm held in a horizontal position and the hand moved up and down denotes Caution or slow down, thus :—

(d) Either arm moved in a circular manner away from the body denotes move away from hand signal, thus :—

(c) Either arm held above the head denotes All Right, thus :—

51. In the absence of flags :—

(a) Both arms raised above the head denotes Danger or stop, thus :—

(NOTE.—When riding on or in a vehicle either arm moved up and down denotes stop.)

HAND SIGNALS

(e) Either arm moved across and towards the body at shoulder level denotes move towards hand signal, thus :—

Above: This view of Charwelton, a layout built by the Wolverhampton Model railway Club in 00 gauge, represents c1956 and shows ex LNER Pacific No 60063 *Isinglass*, at that date the engine was stationed at Leicester, on the Down Master Cutler express. All the carriages are kit built and towards the rear of the train there is a model of an articulated pair of First Class open carriages that were originally built for the pre-war Coronation express service on the East Coast mainline.
Tony Wright, courtesy British Railway Modelling

Right: Westford is a 00 layout built by Gary Stone, and friends, Fenton and Terry, from Taunton. This picture shows the prototype Brush *Falcon* on a Summer Saturday extra train at Westford. I have seen this layout at exhibitions on more than one occasion and I am always impressed with the way it is operated.
Tony Wright, courtesy British Railway Modelling

Appendices

1. Summary of Legislation

The following summarises the legislation relating to the construction and operation of railways. Many other Acts dealt with the setting up of companies, cheap trains, navigable waters, facilities for telegraphs, etc, etc.

1839   Highways Act: companies to maintain level crossing gates.

1840   Regulation of Railways Act: companies to provide returns on traffic and accidents; appointment of Board of Trade Inspectorate.

1842   Regulation of Railways Act: companies to notify BoT of proposed openings; no openings without BoT approval; public road level crossing gates to be kept normally closed across the roadway unless ordered by BoT

1846   Gauge of Railways Act: gauge of any new railway to be standard for Great Britain unless specifically enacted otherwise.

1864   Railways Construction Facilities Act: allowed for branches, deviations, etc, without parliamentary Act if all parties consent

1868   Regulation of Railways Act: communication on trains travelling more than 20 miles; BoT may licence working as light railway where axle loads do not exceed 8 tons and speeds do not exceed 25mph

1871   Regulation of Railways Act: provisions of 1842 Act re notification and BoT approval to apply also to alterations and extensions to existing railways

1873   Regulation of Railways Act: companies to provide annual returns on numerous matters including concentration of signals and point levers, lengths of line worked by various telegraph systems, etc

1878   Railway Returns (Continuous Brakes) Act: companies to make twice-yearly returns on the number of vehicles fitted with the continuous brake

1889   Regulation of Railways Act: BoT may order, with time limit, adoption of block system, interlocking of points and signals, use of continuous brake on all vehicles on passenger trains; subsequently modified to provide for piped vehicles on mixed trains

1896   Light Railways Act: gave BoT power to license light railways (as defined in 1868 Act) in Great Britain, so Parliamentary Act not required; application to Light Railway Commissioners instead.

1900   Railway Employees (Prevention of Accidents) Act: for the better prevention of accidents on railways.

2. References and Sources

Aitken, John *Railway Block Telegraph Regulations* (S. B. Aitken, 1945)
   The Railway Trainmen's Manual (S. B. Aitken, 1935)

Bland, Fred 'A Century of Permanent Way' (paper prepared for the Annual Convention of the Permanent Way Institution, Sheffield, 1925)

British Railway Journal (Wild Swan Publications Ltd), various editions.

'British Railway Track Permanent Way Institution', 1st edition (1943)-6th edition (1993); 7th edition in preparation

Byles, C. B. *The First Principles of Railway Signalling* (The Railway Gazette, 1918)

Challis, W. H. *Principles of the Layout of Signals* (The Institution of Railway Signal Engineers, 1960)

Day, John R. AMInstT and Cooper, B. K. *Railway Signalling Systems* (Frederick Muller Ltd, 1958)

Essery, R. J. *Ashchurch to Barnt Green Line* (Ian Allan, 2002)

Foster, Richard D. *A Pictorial Record of LNWR Signalling* (OPC, 1982)

Hall, Stanley *The History and Development of Railway Signalling in the British Isles* Vol 1 (Friends of the National Railway Museum, 2000)
   BR Signalling Handbook (Ian Allan, 1992)

Hepworth, Wm and Lee, J. Thos *Railway Permanent Way Dimensional Theory and Practice* (Chas Sever, Manchester, 1922)

'Instructions as to the Sighting of Signals' (LMS, 1935)

Johnson, Samuel Waite, Presidential Address to the Institution of Mechanical Engineers, 1898

Kichenside, G. M and Williams, Alan *British Railway Signalling* (Ian Allan, 1963)

Lea, Roger *Steaming up to Sutton* (Westwood Press Publications, 1984)

Lee, Charles E. *The Evolution of Railways* (2nd ed, 1943)

Lewis, L. P. *Railway Signal Engineering (Mechanical)*, 3rd ed 1932, revision of original 1912 ed (P. Kay)

Macauley, John (ed), assisted by Cyril Hall *Modern Railway Working* (Gresham Publishing Co, 1913)

Midland Record No 15, 'Midland Railway level crossings' (Wild Swan Publications Ltd)
   No 18, 'Midland Railway Fencing' (Wild Swan Publications Ltd)

Permanent Way Institution, Journals and Proceedings

Pryer, G. *A Pictorial Record of Southern Signals* (OPC 1977/1999)

Railway Engineer, various editions

Railway Engineers & Contractors (undated but post-1955 catalogue of the Taff Wagon Engineering Co Ltd)

Railway Gazette, various editions

Railway Magazine. 'The Semaphore Signal' by T. S. Lascelles (July-December 1945)

Railway Signalling and Communications (The St Margaret's Technical Press Ltd, London, 1940)

Signalling Study Group *The Signal Box* (OPC 1986/1998)

'Standard Railway Equipment, Permanent Way' (LMS document for staff, 1929)

Vanns, Michael A. *Signalling in the Age of Steam* (Ian Allan, 1995)

Vaughan, Adrian *A Pictorial Record of Great Western Signalling* (OPC, 1973)

Warburton, L. G. *A Pictorial Record of LMS Signals* (OPC, 1972)

Wilson, H. Raynar *Mechanical Railway Signalling* Part 1 (1st ed, 1900)

Wood, L. V. *Bridges for Modellers* (OPC, 1985)

Although not a direct source, I can recommend readers who wish to know more about signalling practice throughout Great Britain to contact the Signalling Record Society.

Left: This two-track diamond crossing was photographed at Widnes Dock Junction in January 1958. An enlargement of the crossing will be found on page 14. *Martin Welch*